"There is no question that Pope Francis loves the saints and admires especially his fellow Jesuits who have been proclaimed saints throughout the ages. They are his guides and mentors who have inspired him along his own journey. I highly recommend Sean Salai's book that offers some unique insights into the mind and heart of this Jesuit Bishop of Rome and introduces us to some of the pope's best friends."

— Fr. Thomas Rosica, C.S.B., English-language media attaché of the Holy See Press Office and CEO of Salt and Light Catholic Media Foundation

"What does Pope Francis think? How does he pray? What is the spirituality that formed him? Good questions all, but now that we find ourselves living in the era of 'fake news,' we dare not trust the online sources to answer these questions. That's why this book is so valuable. *All the Pope's Saints* gives us an insight into the mind, the heart, the prayer, and the spirituality of our beloved pope so that we can be better disciples of Christ ourselves."

— Bishop David Konderla, Diocese of Tulsa

"My favorite order in the priesthood is the Jesuits. They are a dedicated group who truly represent what the Church is about, and as a writer I can appreciate Salai's work and dedication. It's clear he represents the best of the Jesuits."

— William Riead, writer-producer-director of *The Letters: The Untold Story of Mother Teresa*

ALL THE POPE'S SAINTS

THE JESUITS WHO SHAPED POPE FRANCIS

SEAN SALAI, S.J.

Our Sunday Visitor

www.osv.com
Our Sunday Visitor Publishing Division
Our Sunday Visitor, Inc.
Huntington, Indiana 46750

Imprimi Potest:
Very Rev. Ronald A. Mercier, S.J., Provincial
U.S.A. Central and Southern Province of the Society of Jesus

Imprimatur:
✠ Michael C. Barber, S.J.
Bishop of Oakland
November 14, 2016

ABOUT THE AUTHOR

Sean Salai, S.J., is a Jesuit and contributing writer at *America* magazine. He holds an M.Div. from Santa Clara University, an M.A. in Applied Philosophy from Loyola University Chicago, and a B.A. in History from Wabash College. Before entering the Society of Jesus in 2005, he worked as a newspaper reporter.

To Elisabeth and Salvador, Blessings on 9 months of marriage — May the Lord lead you on to many more!

Sean Salai, S.J.

✠ Ad Majorem Dei Gloriam ✠

ACKNOWLEDGMENTS AND DEDICATION

Since no one can write today about Catholic saints, and particularly about Jesuit saints, without relying on someone else's research, I'd like to acknowledge some major sources I've used to write this book. First, I consulted *Jesuit Saints and Martyrs*, by Fr. Joseph Tylenda, S.J., for most of my biographical details and dates. Second, I used the Supplement to the Divine Office of the Society of Jesus for additional biographical information as well as to quote excerpts from saints' writings that appear there as the second reading for Matins (Office of Readings) in the Liturgy of the Hours for their feast days. Third, I used *Hearts on Fire: Praying with Jesuits* to quote various prayers. Fourth, I used Jesuit documents such as the *Constitutions of the Society of Jesus* for the Formula of the Institute ("Jesuit Rule") and other quotations.

For most other sources in this book, particularly for quotations that do not appear in multiple places under public domain, I used in-text citations. I also consulted various lives of the saints and encyclopedias, often uncited, to confirm dates and other information where some sources were unclear. In cases where birth dates or other facts differed in several sources, I chose what seemed best in the Lord. In a special way, I want to thank Joseph McAuley, an assistant editor and colleague at *America*, for editing my first draft. And thank you to St. Athanasius the Great Byzantine Catholic Church in Indianapolis for hosting me while I wrote it.

In addition to these acknowledgments, I wish to dedicate this work to all the holy Jesuits who have preceded me in this least Society of Jesus, from St. Ignatius of Loyola to Pope Francis. Without their blood, sweat, and tears, I would have nothing to write about. It is because of these men that I have often noticed the loving action of Jesus Christ in my life.

Finally, I want to dedicate this book to all the people I have taught as a Jesuit in catechism, grade school, junior high, high school, and university settings. Thank you for the witness you have shown in sharing your own journeys to God. Without you, I would only know the saints from the books we studied in class.

Contents

CHAPTER ONE

IMMERSED IN THE WORLD

And may we be accompanied on our way by the fatherly intercession of St. Ignatius and of all the Jesuit Saints who continue to teach us to do all things, with humility, ad maiorem Dei gloriam, *for the greater glory of our Lord God.*

— Pope Francis, homily on the feast of St. Ignatius of Loyola, July 31, 2013

Desperate and unemployed, the wild-eyed young Spaniard fell to his knees in a cave by the Cardoner River, tears streaming down his face as he begged Jesus to give him a sign.

Convinced by a recent career-ending injury that God was punishing him for years of uncaring selfishness, the young man whipped himself on the back repeatedly, returning to the cave each day for ten months from a flophouse in Manresa where he was staying. His fingernails grew long and nasty, his hair dirty and flowing, but he didn't care — his life had fallen apart.

Fasting to an extreme, the guilt-ridden man ate nothing for days on end, nearly starving himself to death despite the protests of his confessor. Resisting even the smallest comforts, he went barefoot in all seasons. Despite his beard and rags, he wasn't much older than thirty, and he was obsessed with rethinking where his life was headed.

Perhaps if he punished himself enough, the young man thought, it would please his angry image of God and put things back the way they were before the injury that nearly killed him.

Only a year earlier, this same man had been physically fit and happily employed, leading a pleasure-seeking life without a care in the world. The privileged youngest child of a large well-off family, he had never really known what it meant to suffer or to struggle, and he had spent much of his life avoiding people who did. As a worldly soldier in his twenties, he thought he had figured out the recipe for happiness: Take whatever you want from others to satisfy your appetites — just don't get caught. With this attitude, it hadn't taken him long to become a womanizer, a gambler, and a violent brawler.

This way of life had ended in a battle at the city of Pamplona, where an enemy shell shattered his leg. After the injury terminated his military command and left him with a permanent limp, resulting in surgeries that almost killed him, the young captain had spent several months in bed at his family home, slowly recovering his strength and ability to walk. Filled with shame and confusion on his sickbed, he read the life of Christ and the lives of the saints, struggling to understand what God was saying to him through the recent events of his life.

Several questions now haunted him. What did he really want out of life? Why had God let this happen to him? And where would he be in five or ten years if he went back to his old self-seeking habits?

There didn't seem to be any rational answers, let alone easy ones. The young man hadn't spent much of his life thinking about God before Pamplona, but the battle wound and religious books suddenly made his childhood Catholicism feel very meaningful to him. Convinced that his injury was some kind of divine punishment or message, he took a long time to realize God was speaking more through his sufferings than through the vain self-flatteries of his mind.

After getting back on his feet and leaving the care of his family, the young man resigned his military commission, even though his superior insisted he could be promoted to a more comfortable and limited role. Refusing his family's help and sending their money back, he went to the mountaintop Benedictine abbey of Montserrat to renounce his old life and then made his way to the cave at Manresa. At Montserrat he traded his clothing for rags and became a street person, carrying a walking staff as he proceeded to beg from town to town, sleeping under the open sky and in homeless shelters.

In the riverside cave at Manresa, the young man spent several hours a day contemplating the Gospels and the lives of the saints, imagining himself present with Jesus and with holy men like St. Francis of Assisi and St. Dominic. As he prayed in this way with Jesus and with the Lord's saints, different thoughts and feelings came up within him, giving him the signs he sought. Gradually, he discerned that God was inviting him to help others rather than to punish his own body, and he left the cave to begin a new life as a Christian street preacher. Although his family was embarrassed by his behavior, he felt certain for the first time in his life that God was not.

An Unlikely Saint

To his family and friends, St. Ignatius of Loyola (1491–1556) was the most unlikely person in the world to become a canonized Catholic saint, let alone establish a worldwide religious order. But he is the same young man I have just been talking about — a professional soldier whose battlefield encounter with God's grace transformed him from a self-centered playboy into a beggar, a priest, and finally the founder of a religious order that exists to this day: the Jesuits.

While Ignatius may not have been as flagrant a sinner as St. Augustine or St. Paul, his conversion was just as dramatic to those who knew him best. As a symbol of this change in life, he even changed his first name from Íñigo to Ignatius in honor of St. Ignatius of Antioch (A.D. c. 35 – c. 108), the early bishop and Church father who was martyred by being fed to wild beasts. But even though he eventually started the Jesuit order (Society of Jesus) to which Pope Francis, many others, and I belong, St. Ignatius of Loyola spent nearly half of his sixty-five years on earth as the sort of young man respectable people crossed the street to avoid.

Born into the minor nobility as Íñigo López de Loyola in the Basque region of Spain, the youngest of eleven children, Ignatius spent the first three decades of his life as a self-appointed tough guy who rarely darkened the doorway of a church. Professing a basic belief in God and knowledge of popular pieties, he was what we might today call a "cultural Catholic." He was "spiritual but not religious."

For the young St. Ignatius, God was best kept at a distance, locked up somewhere in a family strongbox marked "open in case of emergency." As long as God didn't ask anything of him while he sought his pleasures in life, Íñigo didn't ask anything of God, and he liked it that way. When life was good, he took God for granted and prayed on his own instead of going to church, because he thought he didn't need anyone other than himself. He never considered what might happen if life got difficult.

After reaching maturity, Ignatius joined the military service of a duke, hoping to find personal glory in Spain's expanding global empire during an age of exploration. A self-styled hidalgo, or member of the Spanish nobility, he wore the finest clothing: tight-fitting hose, buckled leather boots, a ruffled shirt, and a gaudy hat with feather on top. This gaudy "look at me" outfit came complete with a buckler, dagger, and sword.

The young Ignatius was Catholic in the sense that many sixteenth-century Spaniards were Catholic, knowing his basic prayers and receiving Communion twice a year. But his faith was completely externalized, being as far from touching his heart as his behavior was from a meaningful relationship with Jesus Christ. His *real* passions involved satisfying his own wild appetites for life, dancing well and talking big, and seeking to impress the ladies at court and in the taverns. At one point, he was jailed briefly for beating up a priest who owed his family some money, but was released on a technicality.

While Ignatius had great desires for worldly success, his romanticized fantasies about life were turned inward, and it would be an understatement to say he was self-obsessed. His awareness of the world started and ended with himself: He was the writer, director, and star of his own heroic epic. But his life, like so many of our lives today, did not turn out the way he scripted it.

By all accounts, he should not have survived his youth, let alone become a saint to whom Jesuit schoolboys would pray before high school football games some five hundred years later. Ignatius was ill-tempered and unstable, a self-styled soldier of fortune who stared people down in public, looking for any excuse to start a fight. Modern historians believe he fathered at least one child out of wedlock, but later genera-tions of Jesuits seem to have scrubbed the records, and Igna-tius himself remains intentionally vague about his early life in his extant writings.

It hardly matters. Like too many of us since the dawn of human history, it's enough to know that St. Ignatius before his conversion was a man who took what he wanted from life without giving a thought to the suffering of others. He was a man who lived by the illusion that he, not God, was in control of his world and his life.

As Ignatius himself summarized his youth in a third-person autobiography, he was a young man "given over to the vanities of the world, and took a special delight in the ex-

ercise of arms, with a great and vain desire of winning glory"
(*Autobiography of St. Ignatius of Loyola*, English translation
by Fr. William J. Young, S.J.). But in a gunshot that echoed
throughout history, all of that changed when the cannonball
smashed his leg during a French military siege at the walled
city of Pamplona in 1521.

After barely surviving a series of barbaric surgeries that
led him to receive the Last Rites, Ignatius reconsidered the
direction of his life on his sickbed, reading the life of Christ
and the lives of the saints during his long medical rehab only
because there were literally no other books in the family castle
to keep his restless mind occupied. Throughout his suffering,
and in the pages of these books, he learned compassion and
began to open his heart to God's healing.

These books told him about the selfless love of Jesus
Christ, but also about the adventures of great saints like Dominic and Francis of Assisi. It was because God's love pierced
his broken heart through their pages that Ignatius gradually
became a penitent, a pilgrim to the Holy Land, and finally a
priest who founded the Society of Jesus under Pope Paul III in
1540. Through its missionary outreach, this Society has gone
on to establish a vast global network of schools for laypeople,
essentially founding modern education as we know it today.

Yet the biggest legacy St. Ignatius left to the world, as
far as he was concerned, was the example of his own life and
spiritual journey as a path to God. Jesus Christ met Ignatius
in his brokenness with mercy and transformed him into a new
man. His life would never be the same.

One story in particular captures for me how dramati-
cally God changed the direction of St. Ignatius's life. Several
years after the cannonball wound of Pamplona, a man who
had known Ignatius in his younger days happened to encounter the saint begging in the streets. Ignatius's changed attitude
shook him deeply. Unable to believe the holy beggar in front

of him and the violent young soldier he had once known were the same person, the distinguished gentleman burst into tears.

Ignatian Spirituality

Today we continue to reap the fruits of St. Ignatius's gift of Ignatian spirituality to the Catholic Church, a way of finding God in the world rather than in withdrawing from it. Through the directed retreat movement inspired by Ignatius, who wrote the Spiritual Exercises (based on notes he jotted down about his experiences in the cave at Manresa) as a manual for retreat directors, we Jesuits have spread this practical spirituality to laypeople and clergy of all Christian backgrounds worldwide for nearly five hundred years.

Ignatian spirituality, as we Jesuits use the term, refers broadly to a particular way of relating to God in prayer, a way rooted in the experiences of Ignatius and the many Jesuit saints who have followed him. It invites people to embrace a Christ-centered vision of reality rather than a self-centered perspective that leads to anxiety and despair. The question that drives an Ignatian worldview isn't "how do I see God?" but "how does God see me?" How does God see my family, friends, and the world around me? What is God doing in the concrete circumstances of my life?

The goal of this kind of reflection is not intellectual knowledge or insight, but "felt knowledge" that burns itself into the heart like a red-hot iron, forging a deep personal bond. Ignatian prayer is like sitting wordlessly before a sunset, savoring what we notice about its presence, and applying it to ourselves in conversation with God; it's not like thinking about the sunset and talking to ourselves about it. It invites us to encounter the living presence of Jesus Christ in prayer, not to remain trapped in our own thoughts. Can I sit with an image of God from Scripture and notice where it stirs me? Can I talk to God about what's really going on inside of me without presenting only my "good" or idealized side to him?

Many ordinary people have valued the Ignatian focus on discerning God's presence in our religious experiences rather than in the clouds of theological abstraction. Despite the reputation of Jesuits for being over-educated, St. Ignatius was a practical mystic whose approach to the spiritual life was based on encountering God in our everyday experiences, not on fleeing from them into intellectual fortresses built on the sand of our mental constructs. Ignatius invites us to bring whatever is happening in our lives to prayer, ask God for what we want, and listen to how the Lord responds.

Following his conversion, St. Ignatius embraced Jesus Christ's call to hate the world, but not in the sense that he rejected God's creation as inherently evil, splitting earth and heaven into two unrelated realities. For St. Ignatius, the Christian who "hates his life in this world" (Jn 12:25) turns away from *selfishness*, but not from the *messiness* of life. So "the world" in this negative sense refers to God's creation as we've corrupted it through our selfish ways rather than to God's creation in and of itself. If Ignatius knew anything from his own experiences, it was the difference between human selfishness and self-giving love.

Fr. Pierre Teilhard de Chardin, S.J. (1881–1955), the French Jesuit geologist and mystic, expresses with particular clarity the Ignatian invitation to embrace God's creation as good:

> In so doing, [the disciple] does not believe he is transgressing the Gospel precept to hate and contemn the world. He does, indeed, despise the world and trample it under foot — but the world that is cultivated for its own sake, the world closed in on

itself, the world of pleasure, the damned portion of the world that falls back and worships itself.

("Mastery of the World and the Kingdom of God" in *Writings in Time of War*, 83–91)

To live in the world without sensing God in it damns us. While St. Ignatius rejected this sinful sense of worldliness in his own life, he was a practical mystic who nevertheless loved all that is good and beautiful in human experience. He rejected "the world" as corrupted by human sin, but he also loved "the world" as God creates, sustains, and calls it — including all of us — to be.

The need to discern prayerfully between creation's goodness as redeemed by the Trinity's saving action (Father, Son, and Holy Spirit working together in collaboration with us for our good) and its distortion by sin continues to inform the spiritual vocabulary of Jesuits today. Pope Francis, the most prominent Jesuit of our time, evokes this Ignatian view of "the world" whenever he preaches about the either-or choice between God and mammon, service and consumerism. He described "the world" in its negative sense in his speech to the poor at Assisi, Italy, lamenting the deaths of more than 360 refugees in a shipwreck:

> Of what must the Church divest herself? Today she must strip herself of a very grave danger, which threatens every person in the Church, everyone: the danger of worldliness. The Christian cannot coexist with the spirit of the world, with the worldliness that leads us to vanity, to arrogance, to pride. And this is an idol; it is not God. It is an idol! And idolatry is the gravest of sins!
>
> (Speech in the Room of Renunciation in the Archbishop's Residence, October 4, 2013)

If the pope calls us to reject worldliness, he also calls us to embrace the spirit of God that lies at the heart of Ignatian spirituality. We find that spirit rooted in the virtue of *humility*, the good habit of seeing ourselves and the realities around us through Christ's eyes rather than through the lens of self-centered distortions. Later in this same speech on the feast of St. Francis of Assisi, the Holy Father distinguished this Christlike humility that forms the hinge of all saintly virtues from the worldly self-interest that makes us oblivious to the suffering of others:

> And Jesus made himself a servant for our sake, and the spirit of the world has nothing to do with this. Today I am here with you. Many of you have been stripped by this callous world that offers no work, no help. To this world it doesn't matter that there are children dying of hunger; it doesn't matter if many families have nothing to eat, do not have the dignity of bringing bread home; it doesn't matter that many people are forced to flee slavery, hunger, and flee in search of freedom. With how much pain, how often don't we see that they meet death, as in Lampedusa; today is a day of tears! The spirit of the world causes these things.
>
> It is unthinkable that a Christian — a true Christian — be it a priest, a sister, a bishop, a cardinal, or a pope, would want to go down this path of worldliness, which is a homicidal attitude. Spiritual worldliness kills! It kills the soul! It kills the person! It kills the Church!

This radical invitation to shift our focus from self-centered to Christ-centered living has not only marked the spirituality of St. Ignatius and Pope Francis, but has influenced many centuries of Christian believers down to the present.

Thanks to the publicity of the global media, it has become particularly visible in the papacy of Francis. Yet over the past five centuries, we can see the characteristic humility of this spirituality at work in countless Jesuit saints and others throughout the world, from the famous to the forgotten.

St. Ignatius and Pope Francis

In a homily on the feast of St. Ignatius Loyola at the Gesu, the Jesuit mother church in Rome, Pope Francis emphasized three hallmarks of Ignatian humility: putting Christ and the Catholic Church at the center; letting ourselves be won over by him in order to serve; and feeling ashamed of our shortcomings and sins so as to be humble in God's eyes and in those of our brothers and sisters.

To help visualize what it means to de-center ourselves and put Jesus Christ at the center of our lives, Francis prayerfully contemplated in his homily the image of the "IHS" seal of the Society of Jesus. This monogram — typically surrounded by a sunburst and featuring the three nails from Christ's crucifixion beneath it — adorns his own papal coat of arms:

> Our Jesuit coat of arms is a monogram bearing the acronym of "*Iesus Hominum Salvator*" (IHS). Each one of you could say to me: we know that very well! But this coat of arms constantly reminds us of a reality we must never forget: the centrality of Christ, for each one of us and for the whole Society which St. Ignatius wanted to call, precisely, "of Jesus" to indicate its point of reference. Moreover, at the beginning of the Spiritual Exercises we also place ourselves before Our Lord Jesus Christ, our Creator and Savior (cf. *EE*, 6).
>
> (Homily on the Feast of St. Ignatius of Loyola, Church of the Gesù, Rome, July 31, 2013)

All the great Jesuit saints, following Ignatius, strove to make Jesus Christ the commander-in-chief of their lives. The Holy Father, recognizing that true humility sees Jesus rather than ourselves at the center of our existence, wants all of us to do the same. Regarding his second point about surrendering oneself to Christ's loving invitation, Francis noted how this humbling dynamic plays out in the conversion experiences of both St. Ignatius and St. Paul:

> Let us look at the experience of St. Paul which was also the experience of St. Ignatius. In the Second Reading which we have just heard, the Apostle wrote: I press on toward the perfection of Christ, because "Christ Jesus has made me his own" (Phil 3:12). For Paul it happened on the road to Damascus, for Ignatius in the Loyola family home, but they have in common a fundamental point: they both let Christ make them his own. I seek Jesus, I serve Jesus because he sought me first, because I was won over by him: and this is the heart of our experience.

In his third point, the pope explores the Ignatian image of "healthy shame" for our sins, by which he means guilt as a natural and healthy response to our hurtful actions, as opposed to psychologically damaging self-hatred. Healthy shame works as a corrective to human egoism:

> We should ask for the grace to be ashamed; shame that comes from the continuous conversation of mercy with him; shame that makes us blush before Jesus Christ; shame that attunes us to the heart of Christ who made himself sin for me; shame that harmonizes each heart through tears and accompanies us in the daily "sequela" of "my Lord."

And this always brings us, as individuals and as the Society, to humility, to living this great virtue. Humility which every day makes us aware that it is not we who build the Kingdom of God but always the Lord's grace which acts within us; a humility that spurs us to put our whole self not into serving ourselves or our own ideas, but into the service of Christ and of the Church, as clay vessels, fragile, inadequate and insufficient, yet which contain an immense treasure that we bear and communicate (cf. 2 Cor 4:7).

Following a Jesuit tradition, Pope Francis preaches "in threes." Here he explores three aspects of humility in Ignatian spirituality: putting Christ at the center, surrendering to Christ's loving service, and feeling healthy shame over sin. But he does not present these aspects as exhaustive of Ignatian spirituality. Instead, he develops them as points for meditation which he sees in the Mass readings for St. Ignatius Day — as images for prayer which strike him as applicable to our own lives. In addition to these points, there are many other virtues in Ignatian spirituality which inform the language of this pope and the way he relates to God.

Spirituality in Action

While many people have noticed the popularity of Pope Francis, few casual observers may realize that the Ignatian spirituality driving his papacy precedes him and will endure long after he is gone. It is the spirituality of St. Ignatius of Loyola that formed Francis, not Francis who formed Ignatian spirituality. If knowing someone's family helps us to know that person, then we must understand Francis as a son of St. Ignatius to appreciate the sources of his spiritual fire, and we must look

at how the Jesuit saints lived to fully grasp how Francis strives
to live.

In this book, I will illustrate the world-focused (rather
than worldly) Ignatian spirituality of Pope Francis through the
stories of great Jesuit saints and their companions. St. Ignatius
notes in his Spiritual Exercises that "love shows itself in deeds
more than in words" (#230). It is likewise my goal in this
book to show Ignatian spirituality *in action* more than just *talk
about it*. Rather than send readers to encyclopedias to look up
Jesuit terminology, or to a theological library for further study,
I hope the lives of the saints covered in this book will speak for
themselves, inspiring readers to grow in virtue and in relationship with the Holy Trinity. Because Ignatian spirituality is first
and foremost about our *experiences* of God, not our theological insights, I want to share the *experiences* of Jesuit saints who
have helped Pope Francis and others grow closer to the Lord.

Although Pope Francis embodies Ignatian spirituality on
a very large stage due to the prominence of his office, there
are many Jesuit saints and non-Jesuit saints (both men and
women) who have lived this spirituality in a less visible way.
The early Jesuits were scrupulous about promoting the canonization of our martyred or saintly members, as St. Ignatius
encouraged his missionaries to always write two letters back to
Rome — one with all the positive details for publicity purpos-
es and one with all the problems for internal use. And the first
Jesuits were forward-thinking in the way they carefully docu-
mented everything: When the Society of Jesus was suppressed
in 1773, the Jesuit archives filled an entire building, while the
Capuchin Franciscan archives barely occupied a single room!

Partly because we Jesuits are such zealous researchers
and writers, the long black line of canonized Jesuit saints now
stretches further than those of many other religious orders:
There are currently about 350 Jesuit servants of God, venera-
bles, blesseds, and saints in the various stages of canonization.

And we observe many common virtues of Ignatian spiritual-ity in the lives of these men, springing from the foundational quality of humility that Pope Francis spoke about. In the next chapters of this book, I will look at the following virtues in some of the most prominent Jesuit saints and their compan-ions:

- **Trust:** *Saints who surrendered themselves profoundly to God*
- **Openness:** *Saints who dreamed big, listened to God, and went outside the box*
- **Generosity:** *Saints who gave without counting the cost*
- **Simplicity:** *Saints who learned to have or not have things, insofar as it served God*
- **Dedication:** *Saints who followed Jesus even when things got tough*
- **Gratitude:** *Saints who saw everything, including them-selves, as a gift from God*

Finally, I will conclude the book with a reflection on the transformation we seek in reading the stories of these holy people, suggesting some takeaways from the lives of the Jesuit saints for our own spiritual lives.

Why does any of this matter? Well, as I hope to show, the Holy Spirit has given us Pope Francis not just for the present time, but for the future as well. He's modeling a particular way of relating to God for all Christians as we progress in our journey through this life to the next. If some readers don't care much for Pope Francis or for his way of speaking about Jesus, they may not like this book very much either, but I hope they will read it in the spirit in which I have written it: with an openness to considering those spiritual influences which have guided the life of Jorge Mario Bergoglio, who we now know as Pope Francis.

Ignatian spirituality calls all of us — not just Jesuits or Catholics — to greater trust, openness, generosity, simplicity, dedication, and gratitude in our relationships with God as we journey through salvation history. Like the Jesuit saints who formed him spiritually, the example of Francis invites all of us to develop Christ-like habits in our lives.

The Gift of Ignatian Spirituality

Having given us a Year of Mercy, and nearing the end of what he foresees as a short papacy, Pope Francis will leave the Catholic Church with the ongoing gift of his Ignatian spirituality — a missionary perspective on discipleship that emphasizes passionate engagement with the world, calling upon Christians to value all that is beautiful and good in God's creation while rejecting all that is selfish and distorted.

From St. Ignatius to Pope Francis himself, this is a spirituality lived by and for hardworking people trying to make it in the world, and it has helped many pilgrims in their life's journey to God. Through the stories of Jesuit saints both famous and obscure, as well as the oft-unsung lives of the heroic men and women who collaborated with them on mission, I hope this book will challenge all Christians to follow Jesus with compassion and renewed energy.

The way Francis has lived out this spirituality, handed down to him by St. Ignatius and his brother Jesuits over the centuries, is distinctively bold and tender at the same time. Jesuit saints often inspire people with their intense fusion of the intellectual and the passionate, the sensitive and the bold. We sons of Ignatius value an integration of mind and heart that continues to attract people in our hectic world, calling all of us to an intelligent orthodoxy that's all about tuning in to the broader culture with sympathy for what's going on, rather than rejecting everything secular out of hand.

My book, then, strives to set the right tone and spirit for a deeper relationship with God. It's about engaging the world in a positive way, but with our eyes wide open to painful realities. St. Ignatius wanted Christians to be immersed in the world, leading our lives boldly and getting our hands dirty. Like Pope Francis telling pastors to "smell like the sheep," embracing the model of a "field hospital" church in which we all find solace, faith, and healing, St. Ignatius didn't want fearful followers praying behind closed doors, safely isolated by creature comforts and clerical privileges from the struggles of ordinary people.

This missionary image of the Catholic Church is not unique to Pope Francis, but distinctive of the Society of Jesus in which he, many others, and I have vowed our lives to God. The message of St. Ignatius is that any person of good will, without reading long theological tomes or taking classes, can hear and speak to God. And the Jesuit saints can show us how to do it.

St. Ignatius of Loyola started his own life as a two-bit "man on the make," seeing very little beyond the end of his nose. By his own telling, he should have died young in a gutter or a brawl, forgotten to history. But he changed the world and became a saint in the process because he woke up to God's love in the nick of time. His story reminds us that Jesus Christ remains active in our world, waiting for us to let him draw us closer into his friendship. We need only to put him in the center, surrender to his invitation, and embrace our reality as loved sinners.

If St. Ignatius could do it, why can't we?

CHAPTER TWO

TRUST

The only really effective apologia for Christianity comes down to two arguments, namely, the saints the Church has produced and the art which has grown in her womb.

— Cardinal Joseph Ratzinger (later Pope Benedict XVI)

Sometimes I don't feel very close to God, but I feel close to the saints who are close to him.

For many dedicated Christians, even Jesuits like me, God can feel abstract and distant at times. Whether we're talking about the Father, Son, or Holy Spirit, it doesn't matter. Because I can't see or touch the Triune God directly, it can be hard for me to sense his presence at certain moments in my life even if I know on an intellectual level that he's there.

All sorts of things can block my relationship with God and keep me from bringing my messy life to him. At times, I may keep God at arm's length simply because I don't want him to see the ugly or broken parts of my soul. Or I may shut him out because I've suffered something awful, preventable or not, that makes me doubt the reality of his goodness.

But even when I don't find it easy to talk with God, I often find it easy to talk with one of his saints, whose deeds and words invariably steer my heart gently back to him. By the example of their trust in God, the saints strengthen my ability to open up to him in trust when nothing else seems to be working.

As high school theology students know, the English word "saint" comes from the Latin *sanctus* for "holy," which in turn comes from the Greek *hagios* for "holy ones." It occurs in

Scripture several times, including the opening address of Paul to the "holy ones" (saints) in Corinth. In this sense, saints include not only all those who are in heaven — whether recognized by the Catholic Church officially or not — but also those on earth who are already leading holy lives.

To become an official saint through the canonization process of the Roman Catholic Church, you have to be dead first. You must die with a reputation for holiness, having lived a life that brought many people around you closer to God. People might then begin praying to you, saving parts of your clothing or body as relics, and telling others about you. Eventually, some people might make formal petition to the local bishop, who would then decide whether to begin the lengthy investigation that could eventually result in you being proclaimed a saint.

The Roman Catholic Church has designated certain canonized saints as "patron saints" with a special connection to various professions, illnesses, nations, and so forth. We pray to these patron saints for certain things in those contexts. For example, St. Joseph was a carpenter, so carpenters and others might pray to him before working with wood. St. Patrick brought the faith to Ireland, so the Irish might invoke him on behalf of their nation.

We also have our individual patron saints. If a boy was baptized Timothy after St. Timothy, then he might pray in a special way to this first-century evangelist and bishop of Ephesus who traveled with St. Paul of Tarsus. The same would be true of a girl baptized Mary, who might pray to the Mother of God for help in doing God's will in a difficult situation.

Patron Saints

You can learn a lot about Catholics by the patron saints each one of us adopts.

Upon being elected Vicar of Christ in 2013, Cardinal Jorge Mario Bergoglio, S.J., chose St. Francis of Assisi as his papal namesake after a fellow cardinal asked him to "remember the poor." Deeply moved by this request, the future Pope Francis recalled the image of the holy beggar who founded the Franciscans and felt drawn to choose him as the patron saint of his papacy. Like St. Ignatius on his sickbed, the world's first Jesuit pope felt especially close to this saint of the poor.

Many of us have more than one saint in our names. My own name is Sean Michael Joseph Ignatius Salai, S.J. Not to the U.S. government, of course, for whom I am merely Sean Michael Salai. But within the Catholic Church, in which I've chosen two of these names for myself, that's my full name.

Sean, my first name, is an Irish form of John. I received it as a baby without any religious significance or Irish ancestry, but I've since adopted St. John the Evangelist as my name saint and December 27 — his feast day — as my *onomastico* or "name day" to celebrate in a special way. In this case, I might have picked another St. John, but I really like John's gospel!

I also received my middle name, Michael, without any particular religious significance. But I associate it with St. Michael the Archangel, the warrior spirit who leads God's army of good angels against Satan's army of rebellious angels (demons) in the Book of Revelation. When I struggle with the demons of my life, I recite the Prayer to St. Michael the Archangel:

St. Michael the Archangel, defend us in battle.
Be our protection against the wickedness and snares of the Devil.
May God rebuke him, we humbly pray,
and do thou, O Prince of the heavenly hosts,
by the divine power of God,
cast into hell Satan, and all the evil spirits,
who prowl about the world seeking the ruin of souls. Amen.

This is a prayer of minor exorcism, offering *protection* (not deliverance from demonic possession) against the influence of evil spirits in our lives, whether they are spirits of temptation and addiction or of compulsion and oppression. At times of internal struggle, no matter how agonizing, I find comfort in reciting these words. As an angel, St. Michael is a pure spirit (he never had a physical body) rather than a human being, so he's not exactly cut from the same cloth as me, but I pray to him when I need courage and help in difficult battles. The image of Michael's winged figure clad in armor and stabbing a demon in the head with his sword, seen in many Catholic statues and paintings, can feel mighty comforting when I want God to stab my selfishness and hardness of heart in the head.

St. Michael casts out the "accuser of our brothers," as the Book of Revelation calls Lucifer (12:10), who condemns us before God as worthy of eternal damnation — this Satan who whispers our sins into our ears to tempt us to despair. Michael drives out the demons of this accuser who tempt us to doubt God's love for us, to doubt our own goodness, and to doubt the evidence of our religious experience and of all created things that testify to God's power. Alcoholics and addicts, policemen and murderers alike, have called on St. Michael for help in times of struggle. I have called on him myself in prison ministry, working from 2014 to 2017 in the Catholic chaplaincy at San Quentin state prison in California, where inmates experience a powerful sense of demonic evil.

My third name, Joseph, is my "confirmation name," a custom from some parts of Europe that has found a home throughout much of the United States. The idea is simple: You pick a saint you like and make his name part of your own when you receive the sacrament of confirmation. It's pretty cool to pick a name for yourself, and often the bishop or priest even uses this name, rather than your birth name, when confirming you.

During my junior year (2001–2002) at all-male Wabash College in Indiana, I chose St. Joseph for my confirmation name after having some trouble deciding whom to pick. Not having grown up Catholic, I wasn't sure how to discern what saint inspired me the most. When I asked our local pastor for advice, he just shrugged and said: "When I was a kid, every Catholic boy picked Joseph." For him, the husband of Mary covered all bases, as St. Joseph is the patron saint of everything from husbands and workers to priests and the universal Church.

When I reflected on St. Joseph in prayer after my confirmation, I found myself admiring his trust in the infancy narrative of Matthew's Gospel, where he takes Mary into his home and follows God silently despite his initial uncertainty. Since I figured I might have a family of my own one day, Joseph seemed like a good patron saint for me, as he was the patron of fathers too. For a year or two, I prayed to him with a little chaplet (corded rope with medal) and prayer that a friend gave me as a confirmation gift. I was also happy that Joseph was the patron saint of workers, as I certainly hoped to find a job after college!

Five years after my confirmation, when God called me to the priesthood instead of marriage, I had the chance to pick another saint's name for my first perpetual vows in the Society of Jesus. Unlike some monastic religious orders where men and women replace their first name with a saint's name, like "Rebecca" becoming "Sister Mary Robert," I was not required to replace "Sean" with another name like "Aloysius" (Thank God!). But I followed the Jesuit option of choosing a devotional vow name, picking "Ignatius" in honor of our religious founder.

Jesuit Vows

During my two years of Jesuit novitiate from 2005 to 2007, I grew to admire St. Ignatius of Loyola for the depth of his relationship with God and for the life story in his autobiography, which moved me to tears and struck a deep chord in my heart. Like St. Ignatius, I felt God's grace had led my life in a different direction than I originally planned, guiding me each step of the way to a deeper trust in the divine will.

On August 15, 2007, the Solemnity of the Assumption of the Blessed Virgin Mary, I ended my two-year Jesuit novitiate by professing my first perpetual vows in the house chapel at St. Charles College in Grand Coteau, Louisiana:

> Almighty and eternal God,
> I, Sean Michael Joseph Ignatius Salai,
> understand how unworthy I am in your divine sight.
> Yet I am strengthened by your infinite compassion
> and mercy,
> and I am moved by the desire to serve you.
> I vow to your divine majesty, before the most holy Virgin
> Mary and the entire heavenly court, perpetual poverty,
> chastity, and obedience in the Society of Jesus.
> I promise that I will enter this same Society to spend
> my life in it forever.
> I understand all these things according to the
> Constitutions of the Society of Jesus.
> Therefore, by your boundless goodness and mercy
> and through the blood of Jesus Christ,
> I humbly ask that you judge this total commitment
> of myself acceptable;
> and, as you have freely given me the desire to make
> this offering,
> so also may you give me the abundant grace
> to fulfill it.
> St. Charles College, Grand Coteau, Louisiana,
> August 15, 2007

Pope Francis, whose behavior as Holy Father continues to manifest the radical trust of a Jesuit's lifelong commitment to God, took these same vows on March 12, 1960, and they sustained him up to his final profession of vows following ordination to the priesthood. They are the same first vows that every Jesuit has professed in various languages since the time of St. Ignatius, whose name now forms part of my own.

All of the saints in my name are part of my life's story. I know them through their relics and writings, through biographies and films like Paolo Dy's 2016 movie *Ignatius of Loyola*, and through my experiences of reflecting on the images of their lives in prayer. And if Pope Benedict XVI is right that the best arguments for Catholicism are its saints and the art it has produced, then the artwork depicting my "name saints" manifests God's love to me in a unique way. In my room, as I write these words, hanging on the wall above my bed are the following icons: St. John the Evangelist, St. Michael the Archangel, St. Joseph, St. Ignatius of Loyola, and Our Lady of the Assumption. Each image has a distinctive iconography or set of artistic features identifying that saint, such as St. Joseph holding the baby Jesus or Mary rising from earth into heaven.

In addition to my icon of Mary, I have a large icon of the Sacred Heart of Jesus, an image dear to our religious order that bears his name. And I have a framed portrait of Pope Francis, the first Jesuit pope who, like many others and me, got to know the great Jesuit saints as he underwent our infamously long training program (it took him eleven years; twelve years for me) in preparation for ordination to the priesthood.

When my life feels like a failure, when I struggle to find God, and when nobody is nearby to talk with me about it, I can always look at these icons and talk with these saints. Their images pull me out of myself and remind me that I am never alone.

Surrendering to God

To live my vocation as a Jesuit, in this day and age, requires a lot of trust. At age twenty-five, I left a career as a newspaper reporter behind, selling a house and giving away a car to enter the Society of Jesus. But in the course of my formation for the priesthood from 2005 to 2017, it helped that I was surrounded by peers who were all making the same commitment, aging and struggling together with me as we grew into our Jesuit lives and priestly vocations.

It also helped that I had my patron saints, both Jesuit and non-Jesuit, to help me grow closer to God in moments of struggle.

On his first All Saints' Day as supreme pontiff, Pope Francis put his finger on what makes the saints so accessible in drawing us to God:

> The Saints are not supermen, nor were they born perfect. They are like us, like each one of us. They are people who, before reaching the glory of heaven, lived normal lives with joys and sorrows, struggles and hopes. What changed their lives? When they recognized God's love, they followed it with all their heart without reserve or hypocrisy. They spent their lives serving others, they endured suffering and adversity without hatred and responded to evil with good, spreading joy and peace.
>
> This is the life of a Saint. Saints are people who for love of God did not put conditions on him in their life; they were not hypocrites; they spent their lives at the service of others. They suffered much adversity but without hate.
>
> (Angelus address, Solemnity of
> All Saints, November 1, 2013)

The saints lead all of us to God through their example of holiness. We may not always believe in God very strongly, but the love of his saints feels hard to ignore. If we believe in the reality of *their* love for God and neighbor, visible in the virtues of *their* lives, it gets easier for us to believe in God's love as the cause of theirs. As St. Ignatius says, when we don't feel any desire to get closer to God, we can at least express a desire *for* the desire.

Even as a Jesuit, there are times in my prayer when communication dries up and I have trouble visualizing God. At these moments, the Father seems to be away in the sky somewhere, sustaining creation. The Spirit appears to be in my heart, inspiring my religious experiences in a way hidden to me. And Jesus, whom outside of prayer I mostly know from the Bible, where his appearance is not described, and from images painted centuries after his death, is "always" with me somehow in a way that often seems vague.

Even when God feels distant or absent, though, I am able to talk with his friends. The saints lived in time and space, like Jesus, but they left clearer human traces in this world than he did. We have their bodies and relics, their personal effects and baptismal records, copies of their high school report cards and writings, and the testimonies of their friends. They lived ordinary lives like I am doing, without rising from the grave or ascending to heaven, and that makes them feel a little closer to my own human reality.

Many of God's friends live among us. They are the saints-to-be in my life who remind me of his presence and love. They are the people close to me in daily life, doing their best to get by in this world. Manifesting God's hands and heart and voice on earth, they make the faith come alive.

All of the saints pray for me, including the long black line of Jesuit saints beginning with Ignatius as well as the saints whose names form part of my own name: Ignatius, John the

Evangelist, Joseph, Michael the Archangel, and Mary (Our Lady of the Assumption). All of these witnesses to faith, living and dead, have helped me entrust the messiness of my life to God in prayer. Just as we have different friends for different areas of our lives, there is a different saint for each virtue I desire and for each issue I struggle to bring before God.

The First Jesuit Saints

St. Ignatius had his own small circle of friends who inspired him and were inspired by him. As he studied for a master's degree in philosophy at the University of Paris following his conversion, Ignatius guided his two young college roommates to greater spiritual freedom by directing them in the Spiritual Exercises. Both of these men, Peter Faber (also known as Pierre Favre) and Francis Xavier, eventually joined him on the list of canonized saints.

St. Peter Faber (1506–1546), a pious Frenchman from rural Savoy who was studying for the priesthood when he met St. Ignatius, was the first recruit for what became the Society of Jesus. Scrupulous and deeply spiritual, he learned to trust in God's merciful love for him through prayer, becoming the first acknowledged master of the Spiritual Exercises. Ignatius, recalling his own scrupulosity, led Faber into a deep awareness of God's love for him as a sinner.

Pope Francis canonized Faber, a personal role model in his life, as a saint in 2014. The pope knew that a peaceful and free surrender to God's will in discernment marked Faber as much as it did Ignatius. In this brief prayer, Faber expresses a trusting desire for God to lead his life:

> Show, O Lord, Thy ways to me,
> and teach me Thy paths.
> Direct me in Thy truth, and teach me;
> for Thou art God my Savior.

For St. Peter Faber, knowing Jesus as his savior was reason enough to trust him, no matter how many unexpected sufferings life brought him. Indeed, when he took ill and died at forty while preparing to attend the Council of Trent in 1546, he passed away in deep tranquility.

St. Francis Xavier (1506–1552), a hedonistic young nobleman from the opposite political fence of Spain from St. Ignatius, was a harder sell than Faber because he was so stubbornly self-seeking. In many ways, Xavier was a throwback to Ignatius's younger days, and it was precisely this strong will that gave Loyola such high hopes for him.

Ignatius liked Xavier so much that he wouldn't leave him alone, hassling him daily with the singsong refrain: "What does it profit a man to gain the whole world and lose his soul?" Finally, during a nocturnal outing, Xavier was scared straight by catching sight of a syphilitic acquaintance dying in the streets. He came to his senses and began to follow the spiritual guidance of Ignatius with enthusiasm, making the Exercises and pledging to do great things.

True to his word, Xavier became the order's first great missionary when Ignatius chose him to replace a Jesuit who couldn't travel to the missions in India. When St. Ignatius asked him to go, Xavier famously responded without hesitation: "Here I am, send me." And St. Francis Xavier left for India knowing he would never again see home, St. Ignatius, or any of his loved ones.

More a man of action than of words, Xavier traveled all over Asia, exploring peoples and places largely unknown to Europeans at the time. He soon ended up in Japan, where Portuguese traders had only recently made contact, pushed farther inland than any European had done up to that point, and established the first Christian missions in a number of fishing villages.

Hearing in Japan of the great Chinese people, Xavier spent the rest of his short life trying to get into that country. But while awaiting a boat to the mainland in 1552, he took ill and died off the southern coast of China on the island of Sancian.

As Xavier's body retraced his missionary steps backward, being carried in public funeral processions at each stop, the crowds hailed him as a saint, and in India one devout Catholic woman bit off his toe to keep as a relic. The Jesuits, of course, made her give it back.

Like St. Joseph in the Gospel of Matthew, summoned by the angel to flee into Egypt with the Holy Family, St. Francis Xavier placed himself entirely in God's hands, walking the fields of Asia with a profound sense of trust in God's protection. There was nobody to translate for him, feed him, or help him understand the cultures he met. He had only his faith in God to drive him.

Recognized later as the greatest missionary since St. Paul, and honored by Christians of all backgrounds, Xavier achieved incredible results because he surrendered to God with a deep intensity known only to the saints. In Asia, he spent every ounce of his energy teaching Catholicism to children and simple persons, reporting so many baptisms at one point that he didn't even have time to recite his breviary. Isolated by cultural differences and by an unreliable mail system from Jesuit headquarters in Rome, he sewed the few letters he received from St. Ignatius into his cassock, keeping them over his heart to feel their friendship more deeply.

St. Francis Xavier's radical trust in God appears especially striking in the Act of Contrition he wrote for himself:

> My God, I love you above all things,
> and I hate and detest with my whole soul the sins
> by which I have offended you,

because they are displeasing in your sight,
who are supremely good and worthy to be loved.
I acknowledge that I should love you
with a love beyond all others,
and that I should try to prove this love to you.
I consider you in my mind as infinitely greater than
everything in the world,
no matter how precious or beautiful.
I therefore firmly and irrevocably resolve never to
consent to offend you
or do anything that may displease your sovereign goodness
and place me in danger of falling from your holy grace,
in which I am fully determined to persevere to my dying
breath. Amen.

As Xavier knew, there will always be things in life which
we hold a bit too tightly, including difficult stuff we don't want
to entrust to God. There will always be attachments that tempt
us to complacency rather than to trust, influencing our sense of
where we're willing to go and what we're willing to do. Many of
us might prefer to put on a happy face and only let God see the
parts of us — the masks — that we let others see in public. But
not talking about our brokenness with God, not being honest
with him or with ourselves, merely hurts us and distances us
from him. And it prevents us from saying to God with the joy-
ful freedom of St. Francis Xavier: "Here I am, send me."

Imagination and the Saints

If we can't be vulnerable with others, we can't truly get to know
them, and those relationships remain on a superficial level. The
same is true of our relationship with God. Ignatian spirituality
invites us to trust God with the ugliest and most intimate parts
of ourselves if we want him to heal us as he healed Loyola, Faber, and Xavier.

The trust that the three companions of Paris shared in God's will for them, from an Ignatian standpoint, is not an intellectual concept. It is rather a deeply felt interior knowledge of God's goodness that arose from their free choice to invite God into the authentic experiences of their hearts. It comes from a firm decision to invite God into our sorrows and joys, into our anger at him for not getting what we want, and into our fear of being our true selves with him. In Ignatian prayer, such a decision typically finds expression in a conscious act of imagination.

As Pope Francis displays in the powerful imagery of his homilies, where he often ponders Biblical scenes like the oil running down the beard of Aaron, we Jesuits like to pray with our imaginations. When I have trouble trusting God in my own life, I often look at the icons on my wall for inspiration, reflecting on the saints both living and dead who form part of my life's story and who persevered at following Jesus Christ in their lifetimes. As my mind begins to focus, I recall to my memory one image of a particular saint I have read about and to whom I have prayed.

Then I reflect on what moves me about this saint and apply it to my own life. For example, I might think about St. Francis Xavier dying alone on an island off the coast of China, clutching his mission crucifix to his chest with the letters of his friend Ignatius sewn into his cassock. As I look more closely at this image, though, I begin to see that Xavier was not alone after all: Jesus was there with him, resting his hand compassionately on the saint's shoulder just as he now longs to rest it on mine. So I talk to Xavier about my own lack of trust and desire to get closer to Christ, asking him to pray for me.

And before long, I find Jesus has drawn close to me again, in spite of my best efforts to push him away.

CHAPTER THREE

OPENNESS

In the end we became one in desire and will, and one in a firm resolve to take up that life which we lead today — we, the present or future members of this Society of which I am unworthy.

— St. Peter Faber, cofounder of the Society of Jesus

Mary Wilson's parents disowned her when she left the Presbyterian Church to become Catholic at age sixteen.

Mary, a sickly Canadian girl from a sheltered family in New London, had traveled with her newly married cousin on a summer honeymoon to St. Louis. Although Mr. and Mrs. Wilson hadn't liked the idea of sending their delicate teenage daughter on this trip, they were used to giving Mary whatever she wanted, and she and the bride were close friends. So when the cousin asked if she and her young husband might take Mary along, Mr. and Mrs. Wilson said yes, thinking "at least it's only for two or three weeks."

After all, what could possibly happen to a sixteen-year-old girl in a few weeks of summer vacation?

While Mary's older cousin and her husband enjoyed their honeymoon, the teenager explored her surroundings and befriended several Catholics, including priests, in the St. Louis neighborhood where she was staying. She found them friendly and prayerful, a far cry from the nasty stories her Calvinist parents had told her about Catholics. Inspired by her new friends, Mary began praying with them and soon asked to receive instruction in their faith.

Caught up in a sense of freedom that she was finally able to be herself, Mary moved fast: Not only did she enter the Catholic Church during her brief time in St. Louis, but she also declared her desire to become a nun.

Her parents, shocked at what they saw as youthful rebellion, refused to support Mary's religious choice or hear anything about a nunnery. They disowned Mary on the spot, cutting her off financially and leaving her in St. Louis to the care of the Catholics she had met. They promised never to speak with her again, perhaps thinking they might scare her into renouncing Catholicism and returning home if they waited long enough.

But Mary, who was made of stronger stuff than the average teen, possessed an iron will within her frail body. Rather than crawl back to her parents in rural Canada, she chose to keep practicing the Catholic faith in St. Louis, staying true to her beliefs. Mary felt she was being open to where God was leading her life and saw her parents as rigid and closed-minded. Her parents, who had done their best to shelter their sickly girl from the outside world prior to this trip, thought she had lost her mind.

Joining the Convent

After Mary turned eighteen in St. Louis, a priest friend suggested that she join the Religious of the Sacred Heart of Jesus (RSCJ) in southern Louisiana, where her parents could not so easily harass her. He also thought the climate might be better for her physically, as Mary's health had been declining ever since the trauma of her parents declaring that she was no longer their daughter.

While Mary was deeply in love with God and desired to follow his will for her life, she remained a sensitive girl who felt tormented by her parents' silent treatment and by their refusal to respect her independence as a person in her own right. So she decided to wait a little before joining the convent, perhaps hoping her parents might soften their attitude.

At age twenty, after not hearing a word from her parents for four years, Mary finally summoned up the courage to travel down to Louisiana, where she soon became a postulant in the RSCJ convent at the Academy of the Sacred Heart, a Catholic girls' school located next to a Jesuit boys' high school in rural Grand Coteau. She arrived one autumn on September 20, still bearing the tremendous strain of feeling punished by her family for choosing her own path in life, and quickly began preparing to take the veil as a novice.

On October 19, the day before Mary was to receive her veil, disaster struck. Feeling intense pains in her stomach and sides, she began hemorrhaging and vomiting blood uncontrollably. The sisters moved her to the infirmary wing of the convent and called a doctor, who monitored her weakening condition as she continued these convulsions for several days, losing all taste for food — including water — by October 25.

A series of visiting doctors concluded that Mary was suffering from a stomach ailment they could not diagnose more precisely. As food and medicine only seemed to cause more spasms and vomiting, they were unable to make her comfortable, and she was in agony for weeks as her body continued to weaken. She suffered so badly that she could not even pray, but the sisters marveled that Mary did not complain about it. They felt helpless to relieve her pain.

On Death's Door

On November 7, after an attempt by nurses to administer solid food to the starving girl triggered a twelve-hour relapse of vomiting and body spasms, the nuns called one of the Jesuit priests from next door to administer the Last Rites to Mary.

She was now hemorrhaging and vomiting blood two or three times daily.

The situation grew increasingly hopeless over the next few days. At the Jesuit priest's suggestion, the convent's Mother Superior asked the community to begin a novena to Blessed John Berchmans, a seventeenth-century Jesuit scholastic (vowed seminarian) who had died at age twenty-two while studying to be a priest. Berchmans already had two miracles ascribed to his intercession.

For nine days, the sisters asked John Berchmans in prayer to intercede with God to cure Mary or at least relieve her uncontrollable suffering. They gave a picture of the young Jesuit to Mary and one of the nuns came every day to recite the novena prayer at the foot of her bed:

> Deign, O Lord, to glorify Thy servant, John Berchmans, by granting some relief to our suffering sister, and if her entire recovery be to the glory of the Sacred Heart of Jesus, grant it to our prayer, through the intercession of Blessed John, that thereby the cause of his canonization may be furthered.

As the novena unfolded from December 6 to December 14, Mary alternated between good days that seemed to get less pleasant and bad days that appeared to grow more severe. Sensing the end was near, she asked the Mother Superior to contact her parents, telling them she loved them and would love them until the end. The girl added that she was happy to be dying in a house of the Religious of the Sacred Heart.

During the novena, Mary lapsed into a high fever, her hands and feet growing cold and tense. Her eyes closed. While she continued to vomit blood, the burning spread from her stomach to her throat and mouth, and her tongue swelled up to the point she could barely talk or be understood. Headaches persisted and intensified.

On the last day of the novena, a Jesuit priest came one more time to administer the Eucharist to Mary, placing a small particle of the consecrated host on her tongue. Mary convulsed in the effort to swallow, uttered a chilling shriek, and collapsed into a peaceful sleep. With nothing more they could do, the sisters left Mary to attend morning Mass in the convent chapel.

By this point, Mary Wilson hadn't eaten solid food in thirty-eight days, consuming only coffee or tea until even that became impossible in this last week. The doctors had stopped giving her medicine two weeks earlier. Everyone, including Mary herself, was waiting for her to die.

An Unexpected Visitor

When the Mother Superior returned to the infirmary after morning Mass, she was shocked to find Mary sitting up in bed smiling, healthy and strong again.

Mary explained excitedly that after receiving Communion, she had asked God, through the intercession of John Berchmans, for "a little relief and health," or at least "patience to the end" with her suffering if recovery wasn't possible.

What happened after this prayer made no sense from a medical perspective, but Mary herself later told the story in a sworn statement:

> Then, placing the image of Blessed Berchmans on my mouth, I said: "If it be true that you can work miracles, I wish you would do something for me. If not, I will not believe in you."
>
> I can say without scruple or fear of offending God: I heard a voice whisper, "Open your mouth." I did so as well as I could. I felt someone, as if put their finger on my tongue, and immediately I was relieved. I then heard a voice say in a distinct and

loud tone: "Sister, you will get the desired habit. Be faithful. Have confidence. Fear not."

I had not yet opened my eyes. I did not know who was by my bedside. I turned round and said aloud: "But, Mother Moran, I am well!"

Then, standing by my bedside, I saw a figure, he held in his hands a cup, and there were some lights near him, at this beautiful sight I was afraid. I closed my eyes and asked: "Is it Blessed Berchmans?" He answered: "Yes, I come by the order of God. Your sufferings are over. Fear not!" For the glory of Blessed John Berchmans, whose name be ever blessed! I deem it my duty to declare here, that from the moment of the cure I never experienced the slightest return of my former ailments. My flesh and strength returned instantaneously, I was able to follow all the exercises of community life from that moment. So that, after two months of cruel suffering and great attenuation of bodily strength from the want of food, I was in an instant restored to perfect health without a moment's convalescence and could eat of everything indiscriminately, I who for thirty-eight days previous could not support a drop of water.

The doctor called to see me that evening, and what was his surprise to see me meet him at the door. He was so overcome that he almost fainted, and Mother, perceiving it, said: "It is you, doctor, who needs a chair!"

The doctor examined Mary, thinking it possible that her symptoms had suddenly improved, which would make sense to him medically. What he found was completely unexpected:

She had no symptoms at all. Her disease had completely vanished without a trace, leaving him unable to explain it.

Delirious or not, truthful or deluded, Mary Wilson was cured. And nobody knew how.

The day after her recovery, December 15, Mary was discharged from the infirmary. She resumed her duties in the convent and received her novice habit on December 17. But one year later she was struck down by a cerebral hemorrhage unrelated to her original stomach illness, dying at age twenty-one. The sisters laid Mary to rest in their convent cemetery.

Before Mary died, the Vatican sent a medical team to investigate her healing. After verifying that Mary's recovery had no scientific explanation, Rome approved it as the final miracle necessary for the canonization of John Berchmans.

At the Academy of the Sacred Heart in Grand Coteau, the sisters later turned their infirmary into a shrine to St. John Berchmans, erecting a high altar on the spot where Sr. Mary Wilson's bed once stood. Paintings on the wall now depict John Berchmans visiting her in bed. In the Society of Jesus, St. John Berchmans became the patron saint of Jesuit scholastics, and we celebrate his feast on November 26.

Grand Coteau

The story I have just told occurred in the 1800s. Mary Wilson (1846–1867) arrived in St. Louis in the summer of 1864 while the Civil War was still going on; Pope Leo XIII canonized St. John Berchmans (1599–1621) as a saint in 1888 because of Mary's miraculous healing. Seventy years after this canonization, Pope Francis entered the Society of Jesus and learned about this Jesuit who became the patron saint of his religious formation between his first vows in 1960 and his priestly ordination in 1969.

To get the above details right in the first part of this chapter, I have paraphrased and quoted from chapter three of *Grand Coteau: The Holy Land of South Louisiana*, by Trent Angers (Lafayette, LA: Acadian House Publishing, 2005), a coffee-table book we received as novices when my vow class entered the Society.

But this story of a sickly young postulant and a long-dead Jesuit seminarian is not merely history for me: The so-called "Miracle of Grand Coteau," the first and, for a long time, the only Vatican-approved miracle on U.S. soil, remains a living part of my story as well.

That's because I lived for two years in the place where this miracle occurred. From 2005 to 2007, as mentioned in the last chapter, I made my novitiate at St. Charles College in Grand Coteau, attending the "boot camp" that all of us — including Pope Francis from 1958 to 1960 — complete at the start of our Jesuit lives before first vows.

We made our thirty-day silent retreat (the Spiritual Exercises in their full form) on the same paths the Jesuits once walked to anoint Mary Wilson. We played basketball in an old carriage house that had been converted from its former use as a stable for the Jesuits to keep their horses. And we celebrated Mass at the shrine of St. John Berchmans each year on his feast, November 26, asking him to help us persevere in our vocations as we prepared for vows.

In this shrine at the girls' school, we knelt in pews on the creaky wood floor of the old infirmary, praying toward the altar with its statue of Berchmans and old paintings of Mary Wilson.

As I write this chapter, I'm holding an old prayer card depicting the profile of baby-faced Berchmans with a halo around his head. I found it in a dusty cabinet during my first year of novitiate. On the back of the card is this Prayer to St. John Berchmans for private use:

John, our brother, you already enjoy the face-to-face vision of God. Please remember us to Him as we struggle here on earth to attain the joy you now possess. Your life on earth was so much like ours in its simplicity and daily round of tasks. Help us to face these heroically and constantly as you did, so that we become daily more pleasing to our Heavenly Father. Amen.

During my twelve-year seminary formation, I recited this prayer to the patron saint of Jesuit scholastics whenever I needed inspiration, just as other Jesuits from Pope Francis to my own time have done. It's a prayer that resonates with my experiences and helps redirect my focus from worldly anxieties to God: John, since you're already "up there" enjoying perfect happiness, please pray for those of us who are still struggling to survive our religious training on earth!

In a religious order that puts you through the mill of up to thirteen years of training for the priesthood, facing the "simplicity and daily round of tasks" certainly invites us Jesuits to respond "heroically and constantly." While religious life and priesthood include moments of joy, our days more often follow a quiet routine that attracts little attention. Jesuit training is so long that it requires continual growth in the patient flexibility that St. John Berchmans exemplified — if you're not at peace with your increasingly complicated life by the time you finish Jesuit formation, you're either behind the curve or you need to start looking for another job.

So yes, St. John Berchmans has been a friend to me, just as he was a friend to Mary Wilson in her illness and to Pope Francis during his eleven years of training for the priesthood. For many Jesuits, his name still resounds at our ordination Masses in the Litany of Saints, even though he seems to be the least-known of the "Jesuit boy saints" — a youthful trinity that includes Aloysius Gonzaga and Stanislaus Kostka.

But who exactly was St. John Berchmans? In many key ways, he was similar to Mary Wilson: Both stood up to their parents to pursue their dreams of entering religious life, got sick, and finally died in their early twenties — John at twenty-two and Mary at twenty-one. I wonder if the RSCJ sisters in Grand Coteau realized the depth of this connection when they started the novena that saved Mary's life.

St. John Berchmans

For someone who has touched so many different people, from a sickly nun in Cajun country to Pope Francis in Argentina, St. John Berchmans lived a short and rather ordinary life. Born to a working-class family in Brebont, Belgium, in 1599, he died in Rome without any great exploits to his name. But he earned a reputation for doing ordinary things with extraordinary passion.

John's father was a shoemaker, and his mother was often ill, so they sent him to live in a parish rectory at age nine, allowing him to attend school and discern the priesthood. After John turned thirteen, his father ran out of money and tried to pull his son out of school to learn a trade, but John's disappointment led a sympathetic priest to take him in as a household servant and pay for the rest of his education. As he continued school in Mechlin, John became a diligent messenger boy, caring for the boarding students and serving at table.

In 1615, when the Jesuits opened a new school at Mechlin, the sixteen-year-old John transferred there. Inspired by his Jesuit teachers, he soon decided to become a Jesuit priest rather than a diocesan priest, shocking his father who expected him to secure a wealthy parish to help support the family. By joining a religious order with a vow of poverty, John would be giving up his finances to the Society of Jesus and could not earn money for himself.

But unlike Mary Wilson's Protestant parents, John's mother and father did not disown him for this decision. They instead reminded John of all they had done for him throughout his life, feeding and providing for him. In reply, the seventeen-year-old John sent them a mature letter that gently but firmly presented his decision as a response to the invitation of Jesus in prayer, not an attack on the family. Comparing how his parents had provided for him to how Jesus had died for him on the cross, John expressed gratitude and refrained from angry accusations as he wrote these difficult but heartfelt words:

> For four months now God has been knocking on the door of my heart but up to now I have to some extent kept it shut against him. Since then I have noticed that during my studies and my relaxation, while I was walking about or doing anything else, the only thought that kept coming to my mind was to wonder what sort of life I ought to adopt. So after many Communions and good works I decided in the end to make a vow to serve God in the religious life, provided he helps me with his grace.
>
> I know that friends and parents are always upset by the departure of those they love. But I look at it in a different way. Supposing that my father and mother were here on the one side, together with my sister and other relatives, and on the other Our God and Lord with his, and I hope, my Blessed Mother; and suppose my parents said, "Dear son, we beg you, do not leave us; we ask this in return for the labors and cares we have endured for your sake...." And suppose Jesus said, "Follow me. I was born for your sake, scourged for you, crowned with thorns and crucified for you. See the five sacred wounds

I suffered for you. Have you forgotten that I have fed your soul with my holy Body and given it my sacred Blood to drink? Are you not ashamed of your lack of gratitude to me?" Dear Father and Mother, whenever I think on this my heart is on fire, and I would wish if I could to enter the religious life on the spot. My mind and heart have no peace until they find their beloved.

I have therefore most willingly decided to offer myself to Christ Jesus and fight his wars in his Society. My only hope is that you will not show yourselves so unreasonable as to set your minds against him.

I commend myself to your holy prayers, and I ask the Lord to grant me perseverance in my intention to the end of my life, and at the end to grant eternal life to you and to me.

Christ's obedient son and yours,

John Berchmans

> (From the second reading for Matins of
> the saint's feast day, in the Supplement to
> the Divine Office for the Society of Jesus)

As John indicates in this letter, he is grateful to his parents for giving him everything his body needs, but should he therefore follow their will over that of Jesus who gives him everything his soul needs? He burns with the desire to enter the Jesuits after four months of praying over it. For many seventeen-year-olds, four months feels like an eternity.

Like Mary Wilson's parents opposing her conversion to Catholicism and her decision to enter a convent, John's parents initially opposed his decision to enter the Jesuits. But while the teenage Mary's parents disowned her, the teenage John's parents gave their blessing after reading his letter.

John entered the Jesuit novitiate in Mechlin on September 24, 1616. A few months later, in December, his mother died and his widowed father entered the diocesan seminary. Ordained a parish priest in April 1618, the father found the vocation he had wanted for his son, which proved ironic since John would never be ordained at all.

God had more surprises in store for the family. After John professed his first perpetual vows on September 25, 1618, he went to Antwerp and then to Rome to study philosophy. Before leaving for Rome, he hoped to visit his recently ordained father, but the elder Berchmans died suddenly before he could go: John, nineteen, was now alone in the world.

In Rome, John did so well in his three years of philosophy studies that the Jesuits asked him to defend the entire course in a public debate. Studying hard for the final exam had already made him ill, but the strain of preparing for the debate on July 8, 1621, weakened him even further. Broken by this strain, he represented the Roman College in yet another debate at the Greek College on August 6. One day later, he suffered the first in a series of dysentery attacks, leaving him with a persistent fever.

After he was moved to the infirmary, John's lungs grew inflamed. But as his health worsened, he spoke to visitors cheerfully about his imminent trip to heaven. The Jesuit community came in procession to administer Viaticum and anoint John, who remained calm while they wept.

Lying in bed, John asked for his vow crucifix, rosary, and copy of the Jesuit rule with the words: "These are the three things most dear to me; with them I willingly die." At 8:30 a.m. on August 13, the bells tolled as he passed away.

At first glance, John Berchmans may not seem like the healthiest patron saint for Jesuits to admire during our priestly formation. After all, he was only twenty-two years old when he "studied himself to death." This relentless work ethic might strike us as perfectionism.

Yet the Jesuits who lived with him in Rome, impressed by John's purity and simplicity as much as by the fact that he had been their brightest philosophy student, were convinced he was a saint. Within a year of his death, they began gathering information to support his cause for canonization. Declared to have lived a life of heroic virtue, John progressed from Servant of God to Venerable, finally being named Blessed in May 1865 — the year before Sr. Mary Wilson said he visited her sickbed in Louisiana.

Sr. Mary, in her suffering, cried out to a Jesuit seminarian who had lived two centuries earlier — but she was calling out to a saint who had struggled with parental disapproval and illness just as she had. In her stifling agony, Mary asked the gentle young man who had died peacefully from a painful illness to grant her some comfort. And St. John Berchmans, in a typical act of self-giving, answered her desperate prayer from beyond the grave.

St. Stanislaus Kostka

Like Pope Francis, St. John Berchmans came from a working class family. But there are two other "Jesuit boy saints" who died even younger than him: St. Stanislaus Kostka and St. Aloysius Gonzaga. Unlike John, Stanislaus and Aloysius came from upper-crust families. Nevertheless, both of them practiced the same kind of determined self-giving that John displayed.

St. Stanislaus Kostka, born into the Polish nobility in 1550, died at eighteen on August 15, 1568 — the feast of the Assumption of Mary — after he had been a Jesuit for less than a year.

When Stanislaus was fourteen, his father enrolled him and his older brother Paul at the new Jesuit school in Vienna. Studious and quiet, Stanislaus prayed often and dressed in

plain clothing that concealed his social status, earning the un-
flattering nickname "the Jesuit" from his older brother.

During an illness in December 1565, Stanislaus prayed
to St. Barbara — the patroness of his sodality group at school
— and saw Mary and the baby Jesus come to him in prayer,
promising he would become a Jesuit.

But when the pious youth recovered and asked the Jesuit provincial in Vienna for approval to enter the Society of
Jesus, he was told to get his parents' permission first. Unlike
the working-class St. John Berchmans, Stanislaus Kostka was
a nobleman, and the Austrian Jesuits didn't want to irritate his
powerful family back in Poland.

Certain that his parents would never approve, Stanislaus
consulted another Jesuit, who urged him to seek out Peter
Canisius (a future saint himself) in Germany for advice. To
say he liked that idea would be an understatement. Early
in the morning of August 10, 1567, the seventeen-year-old
Stanislaus slipped out of his Jesuit boarding school in the rags
of a pilgrim, and walked hundreds of miles to Augsburg!

Canisius, astounded to encounter the youth, could not
send him back alone. Sensing the teenager's sincerity and iron
will, he agreed to admit him to the Jesuit order in Rome. So
from September to October 25, Stanislaus and two Jesuits
walked five hundred miles across the Alps to Rome.

In Rome, the Jesuit superior general (and also future
saint) Francis Borgia — himself the former Duke of Gandia
— received Stanislaus into the novitiate on the recommenda-
tion of Canisius. After four months in the Eternal City, Stanislaus moved into the order of Sant'Andrea, where he lived
another ten months before illness claimed his life.

Although the intense Polish youth put his whole heart
into religious life, he caught a deadly fever on August 10,
1568. Chatting cheerfully with his brother novices after receiving Viaticum and anointing of the sick, he spent the next

five days praying as his condition worsened, finally asking to be placed on the floor for the last night of his life. At 3:00 a.m. on August 15, he died peacefully and was laid to rest in Rome. We celebrate his feast day on November 13.

Despite living as a Jesuit for only ten months, St. Stanislaus Kostka, in 1605, became the first Jesuit ever beatified and was later named the patron saint of Jesuit novices. Like St. John Berchmans, he is remembered for his openness to give his life unreservedly to God in the Jesuit order, even at the risk of defying his parents, and for walking part way across Europe to do it. As many Jesuits have done, Pope Francis prayed to this patron of Jesuit novices and learned the story of his deep openness to God's will during his own novitiate back in 1958–1960.

To be a Jesuit requires this radical openness, in prayer, to know and do God's will at all times. But if St. John Berchmans displayed this openness in a letter to his parents, and St. Stanislaus Kostka showed it in his five-hundred-mile walk to join the Society, then St. Aloysius Gonzaga may be the toughest Jesuit boy saint of all: At twenty-three, Aloysius died while ministering heroically to plague victims in Rome, proving himself open to following God even at the cost of his own life.

St. Aloysius Gonzaga

The eldest son of the Italian marquis of Castiglione, Gonzaga was born on March 9, 1568, while Stanislaus Kostka was still in the midst of his short-lived novitiate. Like Kostka, he was a nobleman, but he didn't have as far to travel in his journey to the Society of Jesus.

Unfortunately, Catholic art has not been kind to this saint, often depicting him as a prissy child. A pampered boy sometimes known as "Little Lord Fauntleroy" among Catholics because of the lace-covered outfits he wears in traditional portraits, St. Aloysius received his first Communion at age twelve from another saint in a moment portrayed by many of the same paintings: St. Charles Borromeo, the reforming cardinal of Milan and council father at Trent. These images commonly show Borromeo, who sometimes aided the Society of Jesus despite not being a Jesuit himself, offering Gonzaga the consecrated host.

Gonzaga was a notoriously pious individual, and one of the Jesuit seminarians who lived with him in Rome had this to say about him. Writing in the house journal about a picnic that day, he recorded something to this effect: "Today we went on a picnic. Aloysius stayed home. A good time was had by all."

Aloysius was also what we might call today a "momma's boy," at least when it came to Our Lady. To be a momma's boy, in addition to being depicted in lace stockings and gifted with the name "Aloysius," hasn't done this saint any favors among Catholic boys today. But in his prayer My Mother, Aloysius speaks in tender words of his longing for Mary's maternal love:

Holy Mary, my Queen, I recommend myself
to your blessed protection and special keeping,
and to the bosom of your mercy,
today and every day and at the hour of my death.
My soul and my body I recommend to you.
I entrust to you my hope and consolation,
my distress and my misery, my life and its termination.
Through your most holy intercession
and through your merits may all my actions
be directed to your will and that of your Son.
Amen.

Yet in spite of his pious reputation, young Aloysius proved to be an iron-willed individual who was not unlike his mentor, the fiercely ascetic Cardinal Borromeo. As a young page and knight in Madrid, the fifteen-year-old Aloysius had moved quickly after finding a Jesuit confessor who inspired

him to think about joining the order. On August 15, 1583 —
once again, the feast of the Assumption — he felt an interior
confirmation from God of his desire to be a Jesuit while praying before an image of Our Lady in the Jesuit church.

Furious that his eldest son wanted to set aside his inheritance to become a priest, the marquis brought him back
to Castiglione, but Aloysius held firm to his desire. Working
to distract his son, the marquis sent him on a dream tour of
the noble courts of Italy, hoping the dazzling halls of power
would make him forget the Society of Jesus. But Aloysius
outlasted his father and finally gave his inheritance to his
younger brother Rudolph in November 1585, entering the
Jesuit novitiate at Sant'Andrea in Rome on the 25th of that
same month.

Matured beyond the level of many novices by his noble
upbringing and education, Aloysius found the novitiate easier
than his pious life beforehand, as his novice master made him
give up various severe penances and fasts he had been practicing. After professing first vows on November 25, 1587, Aloysius received minor orders in early 1588 and advanced straight
to theology studies, where he became a dedicated student.

Despite taking a year off from theology to negotiate peace
between his brother Rudolph and the duke of Mantua, Aloysius persisted in his studies at Rome until early 1591, when
famine and plague broke out across Italy. Dropping his books
immediately, Aloysius waded into the diseased streets, begging
alms for the plague-stricken poor and caring for them. Picking up the dying, he fearlessly carried them to hospitals where
he washed and fed them while preparing them for the sacraments.

Following a very long night at the hospital, Aloysius told
his spiritual director, St. Robert Bellarmine, "I believe my days
are few." Caring for an infected man one day in March, Aloysius indeed caught the plague himself and was confined to bed,

where his condition seesawed as the sores on his body worsened. Clutching his vow crucifix in the presence of two Jesuits who had come to give him Viaticum late one night, he died on June 21, now his feast day. Pope Benedict XIII canonized him together with St. Stanislaus Kostka in 1726, highlighting St. Aloysius Gonzaga as a patron saint of youth.

As a young Jesuit seminarian teaching high school chemistry in Argentina, Jorge Mario Bergoglio, S.J., would have held up Aloysius as a model to his students many years before being elected to the papacy. He would have known that St. Aloysius, far from the delicate flower he appears to be in old paintings, was a youth of heroic strngth. Indeed, St. Aloysius Gonzaga continues to inspire many young people who learn his story in Catholic schools today.

Openness and Youth

In Matthew 18:3, Jesus says that "unless you turn and become like children, you will not enter the kingdom of heaven."

Although a few people mellow with age, many of us become even more fixed in our ways, seeing the world in terms of the past more than through the lens of Christian hope. Growing older, we may cling to outdated ways of doing things and fear the future, limiting how deeply we are willing to listen to God's voice and follow it in new directions.

Even many Jesuits, despite our early fervor in religious life, grow jaded and cynical as we age. Rather than see God's grace continuing to work through physical weakness, we focus excessively on the negative and broken things in our world, convincing ourselves the whole universe somehow mirrors our personal decline. We lose the youthful joy we once found in faith.

But cynicism is not the message of the gospels. As Jesus showed when he suffered the little children to come unto him, it is often youths who are the most open-minded about seeking God without self-consciousness. St. John Berchmans, St. Aloysius Gonzaga, and St. Stanislaus Kostka remind us of what it means to follow God's voice with our eyes fixed hopefully on the future. In his message for the 31st World Youth Day in Krakow, held in July 2016, Pope Francis encouraged young people to open their hearts fearlessly to Christ's love:

> Do not be afraid to look into his eyes, full of infinite love for you. Open yourselves to his merciful gaze, so ready to forgive all your sins. A look from him can change your lives and heal the wounds of your souls. His eyes can quench the thirst that dwells deep in your young hearts, a thirst for love, for peace, for joy and for true happiness. Come to Him and do not be afraid!

In their eagerness to embrace the Lord's call, young people often inspire us to believe in the possibilities older folks have written off. While the wisdom figures among us are invaluable resources of past experience, as Pope Francis reminds us, the young among us are equally valuable in the witness they provide.

Until we leave our parents' homes, our faith (or lack thereof) is really theirs, for better and for worse. At some point, we must choose if and how to live it out for ourselves. Today it's a sad truth that many young people, soured on the joyless witness of adult believers, give up their faith long before they hear God's voice. But other young people have given up their families, inheritances, and lives to know God's will and do it. Some of them have even walked five hundred miles.

CHAPTER FOUR

GENEROSITY

For that staunch saint still prais'd his Master's name
While his crack'd flesh lay hissing on the grate;
Then fail'd the tongue; the poor collapsing frame,
Hung like a wreck that flames not billows beat.

— Gerard Manley Hopkins, S.J., "The Escorial"

In the "First Principle and Foundation" of his Spiritual Exercises, St. Ignatius of Loyola notes that we have received everything from God as a gift, including ourselves. Yet God gives it to us only for a time, to use or not use in growing closer to him during our time on earth. What happens when God asks us to give it all back?

For nearly five hundred years now, we Jesuits have given our lives in missions around the world, dying for our faith in times of persecution, in places ranging from the gallows of Elizabethan England to the terrorized neighborhoods of war-torn Syria. To be a martyr killed for the faith remains a common reality in the stories of many Jesuit saints. That's because Jesuits tend to work on frontiers where others fail or cannot reach — including many places hostile to Catholicism.

But Jesuits are not the only ones who give our lives for Jesus Christ. In a homily on June 30, 2014, Pope Francis made the bold claim that there are more Christian martyrs today than there were in the Roman Empire during the first centuries after Jesus Christ:

> There are many martyrs today, in the Church, many persecuted Christians. Think of the Middle East where Christians must flee persecution, where

Christians are killed. Even those Christians who are forced away in an "elegant" way, with "white gloves": that too is persecution. There are more witnesses, more martyrs in the Church today than there were in the first centuries. So during this Mass, remembering our glorious ancestors, let us think also of our brothers who are persecuted, who suffer and who with their blood are nurturing the seed of so many little Churches that are born. Let us pray for them and for us.

These words of Francis came two months after Islamist terrorists assassinated Fr. Frans van der Lugt, S.J., a seventy-five-year-old Jesuit from the Netherlands, in the Syrian city of Homs where he had worked as a missionary for forty-eight years.

Living in Syria since 1966, Fr. van der Lugt had founded a community center and farm outside of Homs in 1980, giving disabled people a place to work. Beloved by Muslims and Christians alike for his interreligious ministry, he refused a U.N. evacuation order in January 2014 as Homs fell under siege during the Syrian Civil War, staying to tend the sick and hungry. In a series of YouTube videos, Fr. van der Lugt pleaded for international aid to Homs, declaring the following in a January 27 clip translated here from Arabic:

Christians and Muslims are going through a difficult and painful time, and we are faced with many problems. The greatest of these is hunger. People have nothing to eat. There is nothing more painful than watching mothers searching for food for children in the streets.... I will not accept that we die of hunger. I do not accept that we drown in a sea of hunger, letting the waves of death drag us under. We love life, we want to live. And we do not want to sink in a sea of pain and suffering.

In February 2014, *The Economist* reported that the old Jesuit missionary was probably the last European left in the city and had refused to leave "because he was the shepherd of his flock." For several more weeks, Fr. van der Lugt managed to survive while continuing his video appeals. But at 9:30 a.m. on Monday, April 7, Islamic jihadists from the extremist Al-Nusra Front broke into the Jesuit compound and shot the Dutch priest through the head in his garden.

Speaking against the violence in Syria two days later from the Vatican, Pope Francis said the following to a crowd of forty-five thousand people in St. Peter's Square:

> Last Monday in Homs, Syria, the Rev. Fr. Frans van der Lugt was assassinated, a Dutch Jesuit brother of mine, seventy-five years old, who arrived in Syria about fifty years ago; he always did good to all, with gratitude and love, and therefore he was loved and respected by Christians and Muslims.
>
> His brutal murder has filled me with deep pain, and it made me think of a lot of people still suffering and dying in that tormented country, my beloved Syria, already too long in the throes of a bloody conflict, which continues to reap death and destruction. I also think of the many people abducted, both Christians and Muslims, in Syria and in other countries as well, among which are bishops and priests.

Although Fr. van der Lugt is not yet a canonized saint, many Jesuit saints before him have been killed for threatening the status quo. In A.D. 197, the church father Tertullian wrote: "The blood of martyrs is the seed of the Church." If that's true, Jesuits have planted a lot of seeds.

Bl. Miguel Pro

Two of our most famously self-giving Jesuit martyrs include a twentieth-century Mexican with a wicked sense of humor and a sixteenth-century Englishman who suffered a wicked death.

In Mexico, Bl. Miguel Pro (1891–1927) was executed during the anti-Catholic purge of the Plutarco Calles regime, having been blamed for an assassination attempt on the nation's president that he knew nothing about. Fr. Pro wore disguises while he offered the sacraments for people in secret — and often, masquerading as a janitor or street sweeper, he even joked around with the police. The thirty-six-year-old Jesuit had survived for a time with his playful sense of humor, but the authorities eventually caught him, framing him and some of his siblings for an attempt to bomb the Mexican president's car.

Without trial, the government sent Fr. Miguel Pro and several of his brothers before a firing squad on November 23, 1927, now his feast day. As his final request, the young Jesuit asked for a moment to pray quietly. After kneeling, gazing with deep feeling at his crucifix, and silently renewing his self-offering to Christ, Fr. Pro stood up, held his arms out straight to either side of his body, and shouted as the soldiers fired: "*Viva Cristo Rey!*" — Long live Christ the King!

Suffering from painful stomach ulcers for much of his stressful Jesuit life, and living in constant danger, Bl. Miguel Pro did not want to die. Yet he knew the risks and made an effort in his prayer to place himself next to Mary before her son's cross on Calvary. In his Prayer Asking to Stand Near Mary, Fr. Pro says:

Let me spend my life near thee, O Mother,
to keep thee company in thy solitude and deepest grief;
let me feel in my soul the sadness of thine eyes
and the abandonment of thy heart.

On life's highway I do not seek the gladness of Bethlehem;
I do not wish to adore the Infant God in thy virginal hands,
nor to enjoy the winsome presence of Jesus
in thy humble home of Nazareth,
nor to mingle with the angelic choirs in thy glorious
Assumption.

My wish in life is for the jeers and derision of Calvary,
for the slow agony of thy Son,
for the contempt, the disgrace, and infamy of the Cross.
My wish, O most sorrowful Virgin, is to stand near thee,
to strengthen my soul through thy tears,
to complete my offering through thy martyrdom,
to temper my heart through thy solitude,
and to love my God and thy God through my self-sacrifice.

Like many Jesuits whose spirituality revolves around a personal encounter with Jesus Christ in daily prayer, Bl. Miguel Pro discovered a painful but beautiful truth: In times of agonizing pain and sorrow, Jesus himself will comfort us if we generously place ourselves before his cross. No matter how we might wish to be free of pain in our lives, we cannot spend all our days sitting beneath sunny skies with the happy and laughing Jesus, because Jesus himself goes before us to the cross. We cannot rejoice with Jesus at the resurrection until we suffer with him and with his saints, and allow them to suffer with us, at the crucifixion.

St. Edmund Campion

In England, St. Edmund Campion (1540–1580) discovered this same truth as he suffered an agonizing death for Christ during the persecution of Catholics in Elizabethan England. Anticipating freedom of speech by a few centuries, Fr. Campion exercised civil disobedience by writing an open letter to Queen Elizabeth's government ("Challenge to the Privy Council") after he had slipped into England secretly. It spread like wildfire among the persecuted Catholic population.

Mockingly called "Campion's Brag" by Her Majesty's Protestant advisers, who took the author's intention to serve oppressed Catholics and answer Protestant arguments as an act of treason, this bold document is worth quoting in full:

> To the Right Honourable, the Lords of Her Majesty's Privy Council:
>
> Whereas I have come out of Germany and Bohemia, being sent by my superiors, and adventured myself into this noble realm, my dear country, for the glory of God and benefit of souls, I thought it like enough that, in this busy, watchful, and suspicious world, I should either sooner or later be intercepted and stopped of my course.
>
> Wherefore, providing for all events, and uncertain what may become of me, when God shall haply deliver my body into durance, I supposed it needful to put this in writing in a readiness, desiring your good lordships to give it your reading, for to know my cause. This doing, I trust I shall ease you of some labour. For that which otherwise you must have sought for by practice of wit, I do now lay into your hands by plain confession. And to the intent that the whole matter may be conceived in order, and so the better both understood and remembered, I make thereof these nine points or articles, directly, truly and resolutely opening my full enterprise and purpose.
>
> i. I confess that I am (albeit unworthy) a priest of the Catholic Church, and through the great mercy of God vowed now these eight years into the reli-

gion [religious order] of the Society of Jesus. Hereby I have taken upon me a special kind of warfare under the banner of obedience, and also resigned all my interest or possibility of wealth, honour, pleasure, and other worldly felicity.

ii. At the voice of our General, which is to me a warrant from heaven and oracle of Christ, I took my voyage from Prague to Rome (where our General Father is always resident) and from Rome to England, as I might and would have done joyously into any part of Christendom or Heatheness, had I been thereto assigned.

iii. My charge is, of free cost to preach the Gospel, to minister the Sacraments, to instruct the simple, to reform sinners, to confute errors — in brief, to cry alarm spiritual against foul vice and proud ignorance, wherewith many of my dear countrymen are abused.

iv. I never had mind, and am strictly forbidden by our Father that sent me, to deal in any respect with matter of state or policy of this realm, as things which appertain not to my vocation, and from which I gladly restrain and sequester my thoughts.

v. I do ask, to the glory of God, with all humility, and under your correction, three sorts of indifferent and quiet audiences: the first, before your Honours, wherein I will discourse of religion, so far as it toucheth the common weal and your nobilities: the second, whereof I make more account, before the Doctors and Masters and chosen men of both universities, wherein I undertake to avow the faith of our Catholic Church by proofs innumerable — Scriptures, councils, Fathers, history, natural and moral reasons: the third, before the lawyers, spiritual and temporal, wherein I will justify the said faith by the common wisdom of the laws standing yet in force and practice.

vi. I would be loath to speak anything that might sound of any insolent brag or challenge, especially being now as a dead man to this world and willing to put my head under every man's foot, and to kiss the ground they tread upon. Yet I have such courage in avouching the majesty of Jesus my King, and such affiance in his gracious favour, and such assurance in my quarrel, and my evidence so impregnable, and because I know perfectly that no one Protestant, nor all the Protestants living, nor any sect of our adversaries (howsoever they face men down in pulpits, and overrule us in their kingdom of grammarians and unlearned ears) can maintain their doctrine in disputation. I am to sue most humbly and instantly for combat with all and every of them, and the most principal that may be found: protesting that in this trial the better furnished they come, the better welcome they shall be.

vii. And because it hath pleased God to enrich the Queen my Sovereign Lady with notable gifts of nature, learning, and princely education, I do verily trust that if her Highness would vouchsafe her royal person and good attention to such a conference as, in the second part of my fifth article I have motioned, or to a few sermons, which in her or your hearing I am to utter such manifest and fair light by good method and plain dealing may be cast upon these controversies, that possibly her zeal of truth and love of her people shall incline her noble Grace to disfavour some proceedings hurtful to the realm, and procure towards us oppressed more equity.

viii. Moreover I doubt not but you, her Highness's Council, being of such wisdom and discreet
in cases most important, when you shall have heard
these questions of religion opened faithfully, which
many times by our adversaries are huddled up and
confounded, will see upon what substantial grounds
our Catholic Faith is builded, how feeble that side is
which by sway of the time prevaileth against us, and
so at last for your own souls, and for many thousand
souls that depend upon your government, will dis-
countenance error when it is bewrayed [revealed], and
hearken to those who would spend the best blood in
their bodies for your salvation. Many innocent hands
are lifted up to heaven for you daily by those English
students, whose posterity shall never die, which beyond seas, gathering virtue and sufficient knowledge
for the purpose, are determined never to give you
over, but either to win you heaven, or to die upon
your pikes. And touching our Society, be it known
to you that we have made a league — all the Jesuits
in the world, whose succession and multitude must
overreach all the practice of England — cheerfully
to carry the cross you shall lay upon us, and never
to despair your recovery, while we have a man left
to enjoy your Tyburn, or to be racked with your tor-
ments, or consumed with your prisons. The expense
is reckoned, the enterprise is begun; it is of God; it
cannot be withstood. So the faith was planted: So it
must be restored.

ix. If these my offers be refused, and my en-
deavours can take no place, and I, having run thousands of miles to do you good, shall be rewarded
with rigour, I have no more to say but to recommend your case and mine to Almighty God, the

Searcher of Hearts, who send us his grace, and see us at accord before the day of payment, to the end we may at last be friends in heaven, when all injuries shall be forgotten.

Fr. Campion's offer to spill his blood for the government's salvation was quickly tested. The queen's secret police, with the aid of priest hunters and a vast network of spies, scoured the country with ferocity until they captured Fr. Campion. He was eventually tortured, hanged, drawn, and quartered on the orders of Queen Elizabeth, who had made Catholicism illegal and was already executing Jesuits by the wagonload.

The day of St. Edmund Campion's execution lingers in the imagination of many English Catholics even today. After being dragged through the muddy streets of London to Tyburn on December 1, now his feast day, Campion was asked on the scaffold to confess his alleged crime of treason. Unmoved, the Jesuit and former Oxford scholar replied in these simple words:

> I am a Catholic man and a priest; in that faith have I lived and in that faith I intend to die. If you esteem my religion treason, then I am guilty; as for other treason, I never committed any. God is my judge.

Known for his eloquent writing and poetry, St. Edmund Campion had exercised his priestly ministry in England for only thirteen months before being captured. But other English Jesuits quickly joined him in martyrdom, including St. Nicholas Owen, a lay brother who was tortured to death with the names of Jesus and Mary on his lips while refusing to divulge the location of "priest holes" he had constructed in English country homes to hide Catholic clergymen from arrest.

The Jesuit priests St. Edmund Arrowsmith and St. Robert Southwell, a poet who concealed his doctrine in verse, are also among the English Jesuit martyrs. So is St. Thomas Garnet, whose uncle Fr. Henry Garnet, the Jesuit superior in England, was executed two years before him for refusing to break the seal of the confessional during his trial in the Gunpowder Plot under the government of King James I.

Like Bl. Miguel Pro more than three centuries later, St. Edmund Campion saw his death as a necessary consequence of the commitment he had made to follow Christ in the Society of Jesus. He did not wish to die, but he was willing to give himself to Christ in death as he had done in life, in imitation of his savior who had done the same for all mankind out of love. In his prayer A Free Oblation of Self, Campion asked Jesus in his typically incisive prose for the strength to complete his self-offering amidst the sufferings he knew would come to him in England:

> I have made a free oblation of myself
> to your Divine Majesty,
> both of life and of death,
> and I hope that you will give me
> grace and force to perform.
> This is all I desire. Amen.

A zealous spirit of self-giving has inflamed the hearts of many Jesuit martyrs, all over the world, and Pope Francis knows Fathers Pro and Campion from his own formation in the Society of Jesus. Many secular governments have tried and failed to expel Jesuits from their lands, implementing brutal purges that ironically emboldened Catholic resistance by creating heroes for the persecuted. But in seventeenth-century Japan, the setting of filmmaker Martin Scorsese's movie adaptation of the Shūsaku Endō novel *Silence*, the persecution of Jesuit missionaries during that nation's expulsion of foreigners reached unparalleled depths of brutality.

The Japanese Martyrs

For four decades after St. Francis Xavier brought Christianity
to Japan in 1541, the Catholic Church there grew dramatical-
ly, converting hundreds of thousands of people in every social
class, mostly on the southern island of Kyushu and in central
Japan. Several influential Japanese *daimyos* (feudal lords) converted to Catholicism, and Toyotomi Hideyoshi, the powerful daimyo and samurai who became military ruler of Japan,
initially tolerated Catholics.

But on July 25, 1587, Hideyoshi expelled all foreign missionaries from Japan, under pressure from Buddhist leaders
who feared Christianity would become a Trojan horse for Europeans to take over the country, as Spain had recently done in
the Philippines. While some Jesuits obeyed Hideyoshi's edict
to leave the country, most ignored it and did the usual thing
Jesuits do in times of persecution: They went underground
and continued to care for their people in secret, confident that
the edict would not be fully enforced (which it was not at first)
and that the danger would blow over.

Although the Jesuits ministered secretly in peace for a
while, things reached a crisis in October 1596, when a Spanish
galleon on its way from Mexico to Manila was shipwrecked off
Japan's coast. As Japanese officials confiscated the ship's cargo,
one Spanish officer made an impulsive threat that they inter-
preted as revealing an invasion plot. In response, Hideyoshi
ordered the arrest of all the Spanish Franciscans, who had arrived on Japan's shores in 1593 from the Philippines.

While rounding up the Franciscans, Japanese authorities
also arrested the Jesuit scholastics Paul Miki and John de Goto
along with the Jesuit brother James Kisai — all native-born
Japanese men who happened to be under the roof of a Jesuit
house in Osaka when armed men burst through the door on
December 9, 1596. The Japanese government took them first

to the capital city of Miyako, modern-day Kyoto, and imprisoned them with twenty-one others — six foreign-born Franciscans and their fifteen Japanese lay tertiaries.

In the town square on January 3, 1597, the twenty-four prisoners were sentenced to be crucified on a hill overlooking the beaches of Nagasaki. Soldiers cut off their left earlobes as a mark of shame, tied their hands behind them, and proceeded to lead them on a four-week death march to the execution site. At a small village just outside of Nagasaki on February 5, two Jesuit priests met them and heard their confessions. In front of one of these priests in the chapel of St. Lazarus Hospital, Paul Miki renewed his Jesuit vows while John de Goto and James Kisai professed theirs for the first and last time. As the three Jesuits rejoined the procession to the hill of execution later that morning, two Christians who tried to comfort the condemned men on the road were arrested and added to the group, bringing the total number of prisoners to twenty-six.

Upon reaching the hill and seeing their crosses on the ground, the prisoners burst into song, chanting the *Te Deum* as they fell down and embraced the wood. Soldiers tied their bodies to the crosses and put metal bands around their necks to keep their heads up.

John de Goto, age nineteen, had been helping the Jesuits as a lay catechist for four years and was preparing to enter the order when he was arrested. His parents, fleeing from anti-Christian persecution in the Goto islands, had settled in Nagasaki. Catching sight of his father in a crowd of onlookers as the soldiers lifted his cross into its hole, de Goto exhorted him to courage as his father promised to die for the faith, too, if necessary.

James Kisai, sixty-four, had converted to Catholicism as a young man in a village near Okayama. Marrying a Christian convert who gave him a son, he separated from her after she returned to her former Buddhist beliefs. Entrusting their child to a Christian family and going to Osaka, he started working for the Jesuits as a handyman, gradually becoming a porter and guest master.

Paul Miki, the son of a wealthy couple from a village near Osaka, had converted to Christianity when he was four or five and had spent ten years in the Society of Jesus. He was only a few months from priestly ordination when the Japanese arrested him. As he hung on the cross next to his two Jesuit brothers, Miki vindicated the stereotype of smart-aleck Jesuits everywhere: He began to preach a sermon!

Encouraging his listeners to embrace the Catholic faith for which he was dying, Miki forgave his executioner, a samurai warrior standing beneath him with a spear. At a signal, one samurai by each cross jabbed a lance into each martyr's chest, killing Miki first to shut him up and making him the first Japanese religious martyred in the country. As the spear pierced him, Miki called out in Japanese: "Into your hands, O Lord, I commend my spirit!"

Crucified and pierced by a lance on his native soil, St. Paul Miki died on the cross at thirty-three — the same age as Jesus Christ. In the universal church, we celebrate the Feast of St. Paul Miki and Companions on February 6, the day after they were executed.

Silence

In many countries where Jesuits have shed their blood for Christianity over the past five centuries, the crucifixion of twenty-six martyrs on a hill would have been the end of this story. The anti-Catholic government would have collapsed or grown tired of the bloodshed, the Catholic Church would have slowly regained her freedom of worship, and the Jesuits would have gradually resumed their mission.

That's what happened in Reformation England and 1920s Mexico. But it's not what happened in feudal Japan.

In the early 1600s, Japan's military government realized that executing Catholic clergy was only turning them into martyrs — heroes who emboldened Japanese Catholics to stay strong in their faith — rather than discrediting Christianity. So the Tokugawa shogunate (1603–1867), fixated even more strongly than Hideyoshi on rooting out all foreign influence from the islands, banned Christianity outright and came up with a plan far more ruthless than anything pagan Rome or Nazi Germany ever devised: Rather than continue to kill priests, they would torture and kill their own people until the priests gave up.

Going from house to house in Christian villages, Tokugawa authorities proceeded with brutal efficiency. Assembling each family suspected of being Christian, they placed a crudely carved board with an inlaid image of Jesus Christ or Mary (called a "fumi-e") on the floor and ordered each person, from the youngest to the oldest, to step on it. Those who refused to trample on Jesus and Mary were arrested and tortured until they renounced their Catholic faith and became Buddhist. One particularly common torture, "the pit," involved suspending these victims upside-down over a pool of feces and cutting their bodies just lightly enough to bleed slowly until they renounced Christianity or died.

Rather than kill Jesuit priests outright, the Tokugawa authorities now tortured them slowly and threatened to kill Japanese Christian families in front of them if they did not recant. Several Jesuits, brave in the face of their own deaths, were simply unable to watch others die. Under this coercion, some of the priests renounced their Catholic faith, and only God will ever know if their words matched their hearts.

In 1633, Japanese priest hunters captured Fr. Cristóvão Ferreira, S.J., the Portuguese-born provincial superior of the Jesuits in Japan. After hanging above the pit for five hours, Fr. Ferreira renounced Christianity, changed his name to Sawano

Chūan, registered at a Buddhist temple as required by law, and married a Japanese woman who had been widowed with children. He then spent the rest of his life helping the Japanese authorities hunt down and torture the remaining Jesuits in Japan, as well as any native Catholics who still refused to trample on the holy images.

By the end of Shūsaku Endō's 1966 historical novel *Silence*, which is kind of like Graham Greene's *The Power and the Glory* without the happy ending, Ferreira (played by Liam Neeson in the Scorsese film version) and his fellow apostates are living out their days as observant Buddhists under house arrest and constant harassment — but there are hints that these former Jesuits remained Catholic priests in their hearts, doing their best to save lives by cooperating with the government.

After the expulsion of foreigners and the ban on Christianity, Japan descended into a long silence of xenophobic cultural isolation, sealing itself off from the outside world for more than two centuries. Other than merchants who occasionally came ashore to trade, no foreigners were allowed on the country's islands. Without priests, the remaining Japanese Catholics soon became "hidden Christians," conforming outwardly to Buddhist observance while laboring in secret gatherings to preserve Christian beliefs and practices.

Reopening Japan

At the end of this isolationist period, during which not a single Catholic priest set foot in Japan, it was the U.S. Navy that finally reopened Japanese ports to the outside world.

In 1854, Commodore Matthew Perry sailed a fleet of U.S. warships into a Japanese harbor, following up on a previous expedition. Carrying a letter from U.S. President Millard Fillmore in the era of Manifest Destiny, Commodore Perry's ships carried a group of battle-hardened sailors from the Mexican-American War under orders to end Japan's 220-year isolationist policy (*sakoku*) with gunboat diplomacy. On March 8, 1854, Perry landed in Edo Bay, coming ashore with five hundred U.S. sailors and marines as three bands played the "Star-Spangled Banner." The Japanese government, unprepared for the brash American threat, soon yielded to President Fillmore's demands while quietly building gun batteries off the coast of Tokyo and other cities to defend against a possible U.S. invasion. Within three weeks of his arrival, Commodore Perry had negotiated a treaty establishing open trade and a U.S. consulate on Japanese soil.

The end of Japan's policy of isolation also ended the Tokugawa shogunate's political monopoly. In 1867, Japan modernized from a feudal shogunate into a more open economy under the newly installed Meji government. It was this Meji government that lifted the ban on Christianity in 1873.

When the Meji government legalized Christianity, some thirty thousand Japanese citizens emerged from hiding, claiming to be Catholic. They produced black pieces of Jesuit cassocks and rosary beads which they had hidden and passed down to their descendants for more than two centuries.

Questioned by astonished Westerners about how they could be "Catholic" without any priests on their islands, these Japanese "hidden Christians" could say only three things: They were Catholic, they knew the Our Father, and they knew the Hail Mary. They knew these things because of the martyrs.

To Give and Not to Count the Cost

Pope Francis, like every Jesuit in the world, knew the story of the Japanese martyrs — and the Japanese apostates — long before Martin Scorsese made a movie about it. Francis read the book *Silence* and knows all about them. Their story forms part of our DNA as Jesuits, written into our blood with a

sort of indelible mark. It is a story that can never be erased
even if it might be forgotten — a story not unlike that of Fr.
Frans van der Lugt, S.J., and other current-day Jesuits who
continue to die because they are too stubbornly committed to
their ministries to give up in the face of danger.

For a Jesuit and for anyone immersed in Ignatian spirituality, true generosity involves giving until it hurts, not merely
giving when convenient. It means giving one's sweat, tears,
and blood to others in love. It entails following Jesus Christ
not merely in times of joy, but finally to the cross on Gol-
gotha, where God seems absent, even silent.

And yet we have Jesus himself and his apostles — the
first saints — as our models of self-giving for this journey.
We have them as our companions, suffering silently beside us
precisely when we doubt their existence. In the Jesuit order,
we unite ourselves with their self-offering in one of the best-
known prayers attributed to St. Ignatius of Loyola, the Prayer
for Generosity, also known as the Prayer of a Christian Soldier:

> Lord, teach me to be generous.
> Teach me to serve you as you deserve;
> to give and not to count the cost,
> to fight and not to heed the wounds,
> to toil and not to seek for rest,
> to labor and not to ask for reward,
> save that of knowing that I do your will. Amen.

To give and not to count the cost, even if the cost happens to be one's own life, infuses all of Jesuit spirituality. St.
Edmund Campion, Bl. Miguel Pro, St. Paul Miki, and Fr.
Frans van der Lugt all prayed these words many times during
their lifetimes. Pope Francis prays them, too — and so can we.

CHAPTER FIVE

SIMPLICITY

Nowadays the world does not need words, but lives which cannot be explained except through faith and love for Christ's poor.

— Servant of God Pedro Arrupe, S.J., 28th Jesuit superior general

---

For many people who know the Society of Jesus today, "Jesuit poverty" may sometimes feel like an oxymoron at best, a joke at worst.

Nearly five hundred years after our founding in 1540, we own prime real estate around the world, operating a variety of institutions — parishes, schools, universities, retreat houses, social outreaches — in areas which have often grown wealthy and affluent around us. Even with the decline in priestly vocations since Vatican II (1962–1965), we remain the largest religious order for men in the Catholic Church, with more than sixteen thousand members. There is only one Society of Jesus, take it or leave it, and our order has never split into a reformed branch. We have no "second order" of Jesuit sisters or "third order" of vowed lay members, making the sodalities known as Christian Life Communities the closest that laypeople will ever get to being Jesuits.

As missionaries on the cultural and geographical frontiers, we lead complicated lives within the simplicity of our vows. Because Jesuits have a long intellectual formation and are known for educational work, we are particularly vulnerable to the temptation to analyze and talk about poverty rather than experience it firsthand. Like all limited human creatures, we are addicted to our own comfort and are excellent at justifying what we want, whatever it may be.

Sometimes it can feel like we Jesuits express our love for the poor in words more than in deeds. When it comes to illustrating Jesuit poverty in a way that ordinary people can understand, an old self-deprecating expression within the Society perhaps says it best: "We have great, um, *documents*."

Yet St. Ignatius, who founded the Jesuits during the Protestant Reformation at a time when ecclesiastical benefices made many Catholic priests wealthy, insisted firmly on a corporate poverty for his men that shunned fixed revenues and favored simplicity of life. At the start of the Formula of the Institute, the brief "Jesuit rule" approved by Pope Paul III in 1540 and confirmed with some revisions by Pope Julius III in 1550, Ignatius makes poverty — along with obedience and chastity — the means rather than the end of his new religious order:

> Whoever desires to serve as a soldier of God beneath the banner of the cross in our Society, which we desire to be designated by the name of Jesus, and to serve the Lord alone and the Church, his spouse, under the Roman pontiff, the vicar of Christ on earth, should, after a solemn vow of perpetual chastity, poverty and obedience, keep what follows in mind. He is a member of a Society founded chiefly for this purpose: to strive especially for the defense and propagation of the faith and for the progress of souls in Christian life and doctrine, by means of public preaching, lectures, and any other ministration whatsoever of the word of God and further by means of the Spiritual Exercises, the education of children and unlettered persons in Christianity and the spiritual consolation of Christ's faithful through

hearing confessions and administering the other sacraments.

Moreover, he should show himself ready to reconcile the estranged, compassionately assist and serve those who are in prisons or hospitals and, indeed, to perform any other works of charity, according to what will seem expedient for the glory of God and the common good. Furthermore, he should carry out all these works altogether free of charge and without accepting any salary for the labor expended in all the aforementioned activities.

For St. Ignatius, we Jesuits are not poor for our own sake or for the purpose of saying "look at how poor I am" in order to impress others with our Christian authenticity. We are poor in order to help souls, to do whatever we can in bringing people closer to God, accepting only the money we need as communities (not as individuals) to serve God's people. For individual Jesuits, poverty means renouncing all legal ownership of property and cultivating a radical willingness to have or not have personal items insofar as they enable us to preach, teach, and walk with people on their faith journey. We may sometimes need things that allow us to help others, and we may sometimes need to let go of things that prevent us from serving.

For a Jesuit to have or not have a personal cell phone nowadays, for example, will only make sense in the context of his ministry. Back in the summer of 2008, roughly three years into my own Jesuit life, I was studying Spanish at a Jesuit university in El Salvador and felt proud of my religious poverty because I still did not have a cell phone. One day, as several of us were touring the slums of San Salvador, I was surprised to observe that even street people in the poorest slums carried cell phones.

Realizing that my own lack of a cell phone in the twenty-first century had become more of an affectation than a witness, and recalling how many inconveniences I had caused to friends picking me up at airports that no longer had pay phones, I requested permission to get a cell phone after I returned to the United States. Since then I have found cell phones particularly useful in ministry, enabling me to engage people rather than avoid them, and helping me find my way when I'm driving. (Pope Francis, incidentally, had his own cell phone when he was archbishop of Buenos Aires.)

When I taught at Jesuit High School of Tampa in 2010–2014, my new cell phone became indispensable to communicating with colleagues and others at school. Despite my reluctance as a high school alumnus of the class of 1999 to embrace any kind of computer gadget more complex than Microsoft Word, I had to become proficient in iPads and iPhones to employ the tools of my workplace. That meant I had to let go of my personal attachments to certain items — like paper gradebooks and index cards — which I had thought from my own childhood were essential to high school teaching but were actually preventing me from connecting to people in a world that had changed.

A distinctive mark of Jesuit poverty is that we become poor through obedience. Obedience, our primary vow as Jesuits, is so important that many of our priests take a special fourth vow of obedience to the pope — to go wherever he sends us on mission, without hesitation, simply because he believes the needs there are greatest — at our final vows. Unlike most vowed religious, we Jesuits profess these final perpetual vows sometime *after* priestly ordination, and only when the Jesuit general calls us to it. Pope Francis, like many Jesuits throughout the world, professed his obedience to the pope with this formula at his final vow Mass:

I, [name], make my profession, and I promise to Almighty God, in the presence of the Virgin Mother, the whole heavenly court, and all those here present, and to you, Reverend Father [provincial's name], representing the Superior General of the Society of Jesus and his successors and holding the place of God, perpetual poverty, chastity and obedience; and, in conformity with it, special care for the instruction of children, according to the manner of living contained in the apostolic letters of the Society of Jesus and its Constitutions. I further promise a special obedience to the Sovereign Pontiff in regard to the missions according to the same apostolic letters and the Constitutions.

All Jesuits, from St. Ignatius to Pope Francis, have experienced the radical "poverty of relationship" that comes from letting go of everything we know — friends, family, work, comfort, routines, etc. — in order to move to a new place out of obedience and begin our lives all over again. As Jesuits age, this kind of transition remains just as hard for us as for other people, especially if we've been in one place for more than a few years. We are always allowed to *propose* ideas about where we work and what we do, but ultimately our superiors decide where to send us, and we often find ourselves in places — even the papacy — we never imagined. Before we can embrace the reality of a new assignment, we must experience a healthy period of grieving to let go of places and people we've grown to love.

The challenge of Jesuit poverty, in all of these aspects, is that St. Ignatius wants us to *internalize* and properly *order* it to the good of the people we serve in various circumstances. In shunning a poverty of imposed penances and uniform rules that might become its own false idol, allowing Jesuits to appear outwardly poor while remaining superficial inside, St. Ignatius invites us to discern our poverty in prayer and freely choose how to live it authentically. By giving us this responsibility, he not only makes our poverty more complicated, but he leaves a window open for Jesuits to justify our own luxury and complacency in the name of ministry.

In the United States, for example, many Jesuits would sooner take a plane than a bus, or watch Netflix than spend a night singing with people in a homeless shelter. It's easy to tell ourselves that first-world luxuries are necessary for our mental health. And yet Pope Francis, who has called all Catholics to get out of our comfort zones as we go to the margins, routinely took the bus and the train when he was archbishop of Buenos Aires. He befriended homeless people and was a frequent presence in the slums. So how do we, as U.S. Jesuits, maintain contact with the poor while living in a culture that seems to draw us further away from them at every step? How can we live healthy other-centered lives in a self-centered world?

Religious Poverty

Although we try to take credit for a lot of things historical and religious, we Jesuits didn't invent religious poverty. All mendicant, or "begging," religious orders (Dominicans, Franciscans, and Carmelites, for example) and many others require a vow of poverty as one of the three "evangelical counsels" (poverty, chastity, and obedience) we embrace in imitation of Jesus Christ. We choose to live this ideal of radical unselfishness because Jesus himself gave up material possessions, romantic relationships, and control over his own life. Of course, vowed brothers, sisters, and priests are not Jesus, and so we often fall comically short of his example — as did the apostles — but we strive to keep our sense of humor and ask him for help.

Every religious order lives the evangelical counsels differently and emphasizes a particular aspect of following Jesus. Benedictine monks and nuns, like the members of many monastic religious orders dating from late antiquity, take their own three vows — obedience, stability, and conversion of life — which do not include poverty. Yet the Rule of St. Benedict forbids private ownership of property, meaning that individuals must be poor even if a monastery is wealthy. And diocesan secular priests, who spend their ordained lives within a local bishop's diocese (defined geographical region) working in parish ministry, do not make any commitment to poverty at all. Diocesan priests promise obedience and chastity to their bishop at ordination, but own their own property and pay their own taxes, accumulating as much wealth as they like.

The Order of Preachers, called Dominicans after their founder, emphasize itinerant preaching as a form of poverty. And the various orders of Franciscans, rooted in the example of St. Francis of Assisi, whose name Pope Francis adopted to "remember the poor," emphasize living with the poor and being materially poor themselves. The Missionaries of Charity, a twentieth-century congregation of sisters and priests founded by St. Teresa of Calcutta, likewise embrace a radical ideal of actual poverty for their members, who take a special vow to live with "the poorest of the poor."

I have mentioned that Jesuits, with our great *documents* on poverty and notion that "our poverty is obedience," may sometimes grow addicted to personal comfort and admire the idea of helping the poor more than we actually do it. We may cheer on Pope Francis when he shakes up clergy and laypeople to get out of their pews and help the poor, but forget that we are among the people sitting in the pews — or, rather, in the tenured and leather-upholstered faculty lounges of Catholic universities, whose cloisters have long exceeded the kind of comfort diocesan clergy and bishops enjoyed in the time of St. Ignatius.

Of course, I say these things not to condemn or attack my brother Jesuits for the weakness that betides all of us, including me, back to the Garden of Eden, but merely to point out a truth of human nature: We are all addicted to our own comfort and likely to choose it over the good of others, no matter how pressing their needs. We are all quick to ask others to do what we do not want to do ourselves, and religious men and women are no different from ordinary human beings in this temptation.

Our Christian vocations give us opportunities to grow in selflessness after the humble example of Jesus, but also windows for avoidance and self-seeking cloaked in piety. And yet we strive to be "wise as serpents" and "simple as doves," as Jesus exhorts his apostles in Mt 10:16. There are several Jesuit saints in particular who have exemplified this bold and scandalous holy simplicity — *sancta simplicitas* — rooted in the model of Jesus Christ.

St. Alphonsus Rodriguez

In 1571, a thirty-seven-year-old Spanish cloth merchant named Alphonsus Rodriguez knocked on the door of the Society of Jesus, applying for admission to the order as a lay brother. In a series of events that left him heartbroken and despairing, the man's wife and three children had died in quick succession and his business had collapsed. Rather than remarry or spend the rest of his life alone, he wished to dedicate his remaining years to God in religious community.

Fortunately for Alphonsus, social misfits and outcasts ranging from St. Francis of Assisi to Sir Alfred Hitchcock have always found sanctuary in the Catholic Church, and the Jesuits were willing to accommodate his unusual circumstances.

The Spanish Jesuits knew that Alphonsus, who took up the family trade at age twelve when his father died suddenly, had been forced to quit his studies in a Jesuit school to help support his mother and ten siblings. He had met the Society as a child when St. Peter Faber, one of the first companions of St. Ignatius, stayed in the Rodriguez family home during

a preaching tour and prepared young Alphonsus for his first
Communion.

That connection is undoubtedly why Alphonsus turned
to the Society, desperate and full of anxiety, after his family
died and his business failed. With nowhere else to go, he managed to find a home in the Society of Jesus for the rest of his
life. While St. Ignatius founded the Jesuits as a clerical religious order with priesthood as the norm, he also called for
"temporal coadjutors" — vowed lay brothers who spend their
lives praying and working in non-priestly roles — to incorpo-
rate men like Alphonsus into the order.

To be fair, Alphonsus originally asked to be admitted as
a candidate for the priesthood when he was thirty-five years
old and had just lost his family. But the local Jesuits told him
he was too old and did not have enough education, having
dropped out of school so young, to enter the order as a seminarian. They also said his health was too delicate to endure
the hardships of missionary priesthood. So Alphonsus spent
roughly two years in spiritual direction with a Jesuit priest
before finally applying to the Society as a brother.

Br. Alphonsus entered the Jesuit novitiate on January 31,
1571. Six months later, and well before his perpetual profession of the three vows on April 5, 1573, his Spanish superiors
sent him to the town of Palma on the island of Majorca, where
he did odd jobs in the Jesuit college for six years. In 1579
he became the porter of the school, spending the rest of his
life answering the door and chatting with people who passed
through. Palma proved to be his first, last, and only assignment in the Society of Jesus: Br. Alphonsus died there in 1617
at age eighty-four.

Given these bare facts, we might wonder what made Br.
Alphonsus Rodriguez so holy that the Catholic Church later
canonized him as a saint. Aren't Jesuits, as missionaries vowed
to obedience, supposed to move around rather than stay in one

place for forty-six years? Why do we members of the Society of Jesus, Pope Francis included, celebrate this quiet widower as the patron saint of Jesuit brothers each year on October 31, the day of his feast, in our houses when most Americans are celebrating Halloween?

On the surface of it, Br. Alphonsus spent most of his life as a grief-stricken widower who performed the lowliest job in the College of Montesion, answering the door for forty-six years. Today he would be something akin to a high school janitor, overlooked by many. But amidst his simple routine of opening and closing doors, St. Alphonsus Rodriguez developed a deep relationship with God and a gift for spiritual conversation that deeply affected everyone who paused to talk with him. He achieved a serene poverty of spirit incomprehensible to those who have never reconciled their sufferings in God's love.

The Sufferings of Brother Alphonsus

If there's a spiritual poverty for Jesuits sent, again and again, to new places, there is also a spiritual poverty in being asked to stay in one place, and St. Alphonsus Rodriquez observed this latter form of obedience with holy simplicity. Day after day, the bereaved brother was as regular as a clock and as dependable as an old walking stick as he performed his duties, and many people leaned on him for advice.

Every visitor to the school met the smiling brother at the door. Br. Alphonsus showed guests to a parlor before going off to find the student or priest they wanted to see. He delivered messages, ran errands, listened to people's struggles, offered counsel to the troubled, and gave alms to the needy. He wrote that whenever the bell rang, he would imagine God himself standing at the door, and he would call out as he went to answer it: "I'm coming, Lord!"

He found humility and holiness in the dull repetitions of his thankless job running the porter's lodge. When his health started to decline at age sixty-one, his superiors demoted him to assistant and gave him more time to rest and pray, but students and others continued to seek him out for counsel and prayer.

In the Supplement to the Divine Office for the Society of Jesus, we read this excerpt from St. Alphonsus Rodriguez's spiritual writings as the second reading at Matins (Office of Readings) for his feast day, regarding the kind of person he often met at the door:

> It so happens that frequently all this person's business and conversation are with Jesus and the Virgin his most holy Mother, the loves of my soul, and I give them an account of what happens to me. For I really am such a nothing, and coarse and ignorant, that I am good for nothing. And I have recourse to them, giving them an account of what happens to me, asking them to help me and to be favorable to me, so that everything may be done according to their pleasure and not in any other way.
>
> For my heart is full of longings and desires to please God, because of the great love I have for him, by breaking with myself and all my concerns in this life, even with my own self, in order to please God. And because he sees my good desires, and I speak with him and the Virgin, and I want only them and what they want, putting myself and all my own and other people's affairs entirely into their hands, so everything comes out well and according to God.
>
> In dealing with Jesus and Mary I go along with holy fear as I speak with them, and they answer me with gentle sweetness and teach me, by letting me know their holy will so that I can carry it out. In

this sweet familiarity with God and with the Virgin this person's attitude is that of a baby at the breast with its mother; he does not know how to be presumptuous nor is he able to be, because he is a baby.

In this conversation the soul reaches the state, by the grace of God where it does not know how to be — nor even can be — presumptuous, any more than a baby at the breast.

In contrast to his self-description as a coarse and ignorant man, St. Alphonsus felt a lively awareness of God's presence in his spiritual conversations with visitors, and he drew their attention to what the Lord was doing in their lives. Whenever a visitor mentioned Jesus or Mary, he shared his own faith, witnessing to his experiences of them in prayer in a way that would invite his guest to contemplate the holy family. Rather than idle chitchat, Br. Alphonsus practiced his own versions of spiritual direction and pastoral counseling, helping souls who had nobody else to accompany them in their journeys.

The elderly brother's kindness and generosity influenced visitors for many years. In his eighties he grew weak, bent, and thin. Eventually confined to his bed, he was able to attend Mass only occasionally in the last two years of his life. As his memory failed, the names of Jesus and Mary became his prayer. At the end, as the Jesuit community finished reciting their bedside prayers, he kissed the crucifix in his hands and exclaimed "Jesus!" Then he died.

The Prayers of St. Alphonsus Rodriguez

Much of the holy brother's deep prayer life remained hidden to his fellow Jesuits until he died and they found his writings. During his years as doorkeeper, they learned that St. Alphonsus Rodriguez had uttered brief prayers each day that he recorded in his journal. These exclamations helped him get through the tedium of his job by turning it into a prayer.

Fr. Michael Harter, S.J., has reprinted the English translation of several prayers by this saint in his edited collection *Hearts on Fire: Praying with Jesuits.* Here we find that one of St. Alphonsus Rodriguez's favorite exclamations was "Lord, show me the way." Others included "Lord, you do your will and not mine" and "Lord, let me know you, let me know myself."

But Br. Alphonsus also recorded some longer prayers as he drew closer to the crucified Lord in the midst of his sufferings, including this Prayer to Seek the Consolation of the Cross:

Jesus, lover of my soul, center of my heart!
Why am I not more eager
to endure pains and tribulations for love of you,
when you, my God, have suffered so many for me?

Come, then, every sort of trial in the world,
for this is my delight, to suffer for Jesus.
This is my joy, to follow my Savior,
and to find my consolation
with my consoler on the cross.

This is my happiness, this is my pleasure:
to live with Jesus, to walk with Jesus, to converse with Jesus;
to suffer with and for him,
this is my treasure.

Here we find the single-minded focus on Jesus Christ in the midst of daily life that gives Ignatian spirituality much of its flavor. Tasked with the simple job of opening and closing the front door at a Jesuit school, St. Alphonsus Rodriguez waited each day for Jesus to walk through the door, and he offered his sufferings to the crucified God made man. Like Pope Francis, he found deep meaning in his day and in everyone he met because he sought consciously to find Jesus personally present in each and every moment of each and every hour.

By paying attention to the presence of Jesus in the middle of his routine, Br. Alphonsus found peace and a new lease on life. His way of praying was so simple that many of us might never dare try it: He just thought about Jesus all the time, inviting the Lord into his thoughts and feelings in a way that forged a deep inner relationship. In his Prayer for New Life through Death to Sin, we see how he practiced this virtue in the way he spoke to Jesus:

> Through your most holy passion and death,
> I beg of you, Lord, to grant me a most holy life,
> and a most complete death to all my vices
> and passions and self-love,
> and to grant me sight of your holy faith, hope, and charity.

For this man who had lost his wife, children, and career, the suffering and death of Jesus was particularly vivid. His ability to offer Christ the most broken parts of himself brought him tremendous healing and joy.

It may seem difficult to capture the holiness of such a quiet and inwardly focused saint. But in the late nineteenth century, Fr. Gerard Manley Hopkins, S.J., the English Jesuit poet, tried to catch the spirit of Br. Alphonsus in this poem:

> In honour of St. Alphonsus Rodriguez
> Laybrother of the Society of Jesus

> HONOUR is flashed off exploit, so we say;
> And those strokes once that gashed flesh or galled shield
> Should tongue that time now, trumpet now that field,
> And, on the fighter, forge his glorious day.
> On Christ they do and on the martyr may;
> But be the war within, the brand we wield
> Unseen, the heroic breast not outward-steeled,

Earth hears no hurtle then from fiercest fray.
Yet God (that hews mountain and continent,
Earth, all, out; who, with trickling increment,
Veins violets and tall trees makes more and more)
Could crowd career with conquest while there went
Those years and years by of world without event
That in Majorca Alfonso watched the door.

In this poem, Hopkins bathes Rodriguez in an image of glory forged in the quiet heroism of loving God and loving neighbor, a victory achieved through the interior battle of a soul surrendering to Jesus rather than seeking the pomp of earthly fame. To spend many decades faithfully answering a door may not seem as impressive as a glorious and bloody martyrdom, yet Hopkins believed this faithful way of life, offered to God amid one's daily activities, represents its own kind of martyrdom.

When his fellow Jesuits discovered the deep prayer life hidden in Br. Alphonsus's journals after he died, they put their beloved doorkeeper on the road to canonized sainthood in the Catholic Church. But the elderly brother had achieved one other thing that was not so hidden: When he was seventy-two, Alphonsus influenced the path of another Jesuit saint, sending him on a mission across the world that reached far beyond the doors of his little school.

St. Peter Claver

In 1605, a twenty-five-year-old Jesuit scholastic named Peter Claver (1580–1654) came for his philosophy studies to the College of Montesion, filled with the desire to do something great for God but unsure of where to start. Striking up a friendship with Br. Alphonsus, he often walked the grounds with the doorkeeper to discuss prayer and growth in the spiritual life. Over the course of three years, this friendship changed the seminarian's life forever.

Born to a wealthy farmer in Catalonia as the youngest of four children, Peter Claver met the Jesuits during university studies in Barcelona, entering the order at twenty-two and taking his three vows on August 8, 1604. Like many Jesuit seminarians then and now, he entered philosophy studies full of angst and uncertainty about what he would do as a Jesuit priest. But having already heard of the holy Br. Alphonsus, he looked forward to consulting the porter about how to spend his life in the Society.

Sharing the secret of his own prayer life, St. Alphonsus Rodriguez gave young Peter a simple piece of advice: "Look for God in all men and serve them as images of him." Sensing Peter's great desire to make a difference in the world, the holy brother spoke to him about the need for missionaries in the New World, asking him: "Why don't you go there yourself and bring souls to Jesus Christ?"

Impressed by this idea, Peter prayed over it and asked his superiors for permission to go, but they didn't answer him right away. In 1608, he was assigned to study theology in Barcelona, where his request was finally answered two years later by a letter from his provincial superior: The provincial had granted his request. He instructed Peter to sail from Spain to the Caribbean port of Cartagena in present-day Colombia, where he would work in the Spanish colonies of the New World.

From July 1610 to November 1615, Peter finished his theological studies at the Jesuit college in Bogota, then settled into Cartagena to minister in the port. Here was ordained a priest at age thirty-six — the first Jesuit ordained in Cartagena — on March 19, 1616.

Fr. Claver soon discovered the unpleasant realities of Cartagena, one of two Spanish-American ports receiving slaves from West Africa that processed an average of ten thousand per year. Rather than work with the wealthy and powerful, Claver started going to these slaves each day with fruits and baked goods he begged in the city. Descending into the windowless hold of each arriving slave ship, where typically only two-thirds of the half-dead Africans survived the months-long voyage, Fr. Claver spoke to them through interpreters who had been former slaves themselves. Offering food from his baskets and embracing them, he vowed to become "the slave of the slaves forever."

Like St. Alphonsus Rodriguez at the door in Palma, Fr. Claver spent the rest of his life on the miserable docks of Cartagena, possessing only what he needed to fulfill his ministry and nothing more — it became his first, last, and only priestly assignment in the Society of Jesus. Cleaning and bandaging the sick in the slave ships, and sometimes bringing a second Jesuit priest with him, he strove to offer the Africans a face of kindness rather than a look of cruelty, speaking briefly to each one about God and ultimately baptizing an estimated three hundred thousand people in his four decades there. As each cargo hold was unloaded and the slaves were housed in sheds built on the docks, he continued to visit them daily until they were sold and transported to other cities.

In the second reading for Matins on his feast day in the Jesuit Supplement to the Divine Office, this excerpt from a letter of St. Peter Claver to his Jesuit superior describes what he experienced in his rounds among the slave huts of the docks:

> *To bring good tidings to the poor, to bind up the broken-hearted, to proclaim liberty to the captives (cf. Is. 61:1).*
>
> Yesterday, May 30, 1627, the feast of the Most Holy Trinity, a great number of black people who had been seized from along the African rivers were put ashore from one very large vessel. We hurried

out with two baskets full of oranges, lemons, sweet biscuits, and all sorts of other things.

When we reached their huts it was like entering another Guinea. We had to force our way through the crowds till we reached the sick. There was a great number of them, lying on the damp earth, or rather in mud; but someone had formed the idea of making a heap of tiles and broken bricks in case the damp should be too much for them. This was all they had for a bed, all the more uncomfortable because they were naked, without any covering at all.

We took off our cloaks, went to a store, bought from there all the wood that was available and put it together to make a platform; then, forcing a way through the guards, we eventually managed to carry all the sick onto it. Then we separated them into two groups; one of them my companion addressed with the aid of an interpreter, the other I spoke to myself.

Two of the black slaves were more dead than alive; they were already cold, and we could hardly feel any pulse in their veins. We got together some glowing embers on a tile, placed the dying men near them, and then threw aromatic spices on the fire. We had two bags of these spices, and used them all. Then with the help of our cloaks — for the slaves had none of their own, and it would have been a waste of time to ask their masters — we got them to inhale the vapors, which seemed to restore their warmth and vitality. You should have seen the expression of gratitude in their eyes!

In this way we spoke to them, not with words but with deeds; and for people in their situation who were convinced that they had been brought there to be eaten, any other form of address would have been pointless. Then we sat or knelt beside them and washed their faces and bodies with wine; by such acts of kindness we tried to cheer them up, and performed for them all the natural services which are calculated to raise the spirits of the sick.

Then we began to instruct them for baptism. We first explained to them the wonderful effects of the sacrament on both body and soul, and when they showed by their answers to our questions that they understood us sufficiently well, we began to teach them at greater length concerning the one God who rewards and punishes each according to his deserts, and so on. We urged them to repent and give some indication of sorrow for their sins.

Finally, when they seemed to be sufficiently prepared, we explained to them the mysteries of the Trinity, Incarnation, and Passion. We showed them a representation of Christ crucified above a baptismal font, into which the blood flowed from his wounds. Then we taught them to repeat after us the act of contrition in their own language.

As we see in this letter, St. Peter Claver cared for the slaves in body and soul, baptizing them into Christianity and sharing his faith in a fraternal way that challenged the status quo among wealthy Spanish colonists who viewed the Africans as subhuman, not deserving of the equal rights conferred by baptism on children of God. Unable to speak the language of the slaves, Claver lived out the maxim of St. Ignatius to show his love in deeds more than in words.

It might seem easy for us today, with our distance from seventeenth-century values, to misjudge the saint's motives as condescending or paternalistic. Looking back at this letter through a sophisticated twenty-first-century lens, we may be tempted to view Fr. Claver's simplicity as simplistic rather than forward-looking. And yet there is no denying he loved the poor.

Love for the Poor

In some Catholic social justice circles since the Second Vatican Council, it has become common to criticize organized charity as a bandage that merely *relieves* human suffering while leaving in place the unjust social structures that *cause* it. At the same time, this analytical stance can make it easy for Catholics to complain about poverty in an abstract sense, treating it as a statistical problem to be addressed by politicians while we stare straight ahead and walk past homeless people on the streets each day.

Rather than love God and neighbor as Claver did, we may prefer to get angry at others for *not* doing it, stewing in our own self-righteousness. Instead of putting our faith in Jesus Christ, his saints, and the Gospels, we might profess our belief in the Republicans, the Democrats, or the *New York Times*. Rather than help the poor ourselves, we may expect others to do it while we struggle for our own survival in an economic system that increasingly concentrates wealth and power in the hands of a few.

In our affluent United States, where Catholics now comprise the wealthiest and most educated segment of the population, we might even find ourselves using social justice rhetoric to justify our own comfort, outsourcing actual charity to others while we build lives for ourselves in comfortable enclaves removed from human suffering. Forgetting our working-class roots, including the immigrants among us today, we might use social justice language to avoid direct encounters with the poor as easily as we might use charity to avoid asking the question of why the poor are poor. In an unjust world, we may too easily surrender to the temptation to isolate ourselves, arguing from our armchairs and coffee shops about "first world problems" while real people suffer and die in the slave ships of our age.

Yet Pope Francis, who as a South American Jesuit is quite familiar with St. Peter Claver's work on his continent, has firmly rejected the idea that it's okay for Catholics to "work for justice" through words rather than deeds, that it's enough to write angry political tracts from the ivory towers of Catholic universities while avoiding the poor. Charity remains a particular necessity for all Catholics, not merely the task of the few among us who seem willing to forfeit material gains. At an evening prayer vigil for Divine Mercy Sunday on April 2, 2016, during the Jubilee Year of Mercy, Pope Francis said we actually need *more* charity:

> As a reminder, a "monument" let's say, to this Year of Mercy, how beautiful it would be if in every diocese there were a structural work of mercy: a hospital, a home for the aged or abandoned children, a school where there isn't one, a home for recovering drug addicts — so many things could be done.

In the spirit of these words, St. Peter Claver appears to be a Jesuit saint after the pope's own heart — a humble priest of rich compassion who waded into unthinkable poverty without fear, getting his hands dirty rather than remaining safely entrenched behind church walls. Even in our complicated age, this kind of love shows itself more in deeds than in words, through the simple acts of kindness that seem far too easy for us to avoid.

The Death of St. Peter Claver

In the last five years of his life, Fr. Claver experienced a deepening poverty of body and soul that made his simple life even simpler, allowing him to share the poverty of the slaves in a surprising way. Although there was no such thing as a "day off" for Claver, he ended up bedridden in 1650 after caring for plague victims and catching the disease himself.

With many Jesuits in Cartagena also stricken by the plague, they hired a former slave to care for St. Peter Claver, but the man abused him, eating his food and refusing to bathe him. Reduced to helpless dependence, Claver could not celebrate Mass or hear confessions for the last four years of his life, and he rarely got out of bed. Instead, he placed himself in the Lord's hands, reckoning that he deserved the abuse he was receiving in reparation for the abuse the slaves had suffered.

When Fr. Claver finally received the anointing of the sick, the slaves and citizens of Cartagena flocked to his room, stripping it of everything except the bed clothes to keep as a relic of the holy man. Sometime between 1:00 and 2:00 a.m. on the Feast of the Nativity of Our Lord, 1654, he became unconscious and died peacefully in his sleep at age seventy-four. In 1888, Pope Leo XIII canonized Peter Claver together with his friend Alphonsus Rodriguez, who had first encouraged him to go to the New World.

Although many Catholics outside of Jesuit circles do not know the story of St. Peter Claver, whose September 9 feast day is a memorial in the United States, Pope Leo XIII declared him the special patron of missions to the black peoples of the world — and many African-American Catholics continue to celebrate him today with special fondness.

During my Jesuit novitiate in Louisiana, I met the Knights of St. Peter Claver, a primarily African-American Catholic service fraternity — especially active in the Southern United States, they are sometimes described as "the black Knights of Columbus." Meeting in their hall at St. Charles Borromeo Catholic Church, the Jesuit parish in Grand Coteau, the Knights provided for the needy in our predominantly black and Catholic community. They staged cultural and other community events, impressing me with their commitment to continue the work of this saint on behalf of black people throughout the world.

A small icon that I've kept on my wall for many years depicts St. Peter Claver standing in his Jesuit cassock, holding a black child in one arm and surrounded by parrots. As the child looks at the Jesuit and holds a finger to his own lips, Fr. Claver points to the child with his free hand. But the saint is not looking at the child — his eyes stare out at *us* rather than at the child.

At first glance, it seems unclear whether the child represents a slave, an African depiction of Jesus Christ, or both. But if one looks at it with the eyes of faith, the answer begins to come into focus. And I'm pretty sure Br. Alphonsus and Fr. Claver would know it.

CHAPTER SIX

DEDICATION

You, when wild sects tortured and mocked each other,
Saw truth in the wild tribes that tortured you;
Slurred for not slurring all who slurred or slew,
Blamed that your murderer was too much your brother.

— G.K. Chesterton, "To the Jesuits"

In 1675, French Jesuit missionaries in upstate New York baptized a nineteen-year-old Algonquin-Mohawk girl named Tekakwitha, giving her the Christian name "Catherine" in honor of the great Dominican nun St. Catherine of Siena.

This American Indian teenager had suffered a rough life, losing her parents and baby brother to a smallpox epidemic that permanently scarred her face when she was four years old. Battles with other Indian tribes and with French soldiers later displaced her from her birth village of Ossernenon on the south side of the Mohawk River west of modern-day Auriesville. Yet the Jesuit missionaries, learning the native tongues and translating the Our Father into Mohawk, presented Christianity as something that appealed to her.

They learned Tekakwitha (1656–1680) had been born into a life of violence and coercion: Her Algonquin birth mother had been baptized Roman Catholic before being captured by the Iroquois and given as a trophy wife to the fierce chief of the Mohawk clan, Tekakwitha's birth father. As the Jesuits shared their faith, the Catholic esteem for virginity appealed deeply to the teenaged Kateri (the Mohawk form of "Catherine") because her adoptive parents and aunts had tried several times to force her into arranged marriages with Mohawk warriors, punishing her with verbal, physical, and emotional abuse for refusing to enter wedlock from the time she turned thirteen.

The Jesuits, three of whom lodged with the girl's uncle and were known as "Black Robes" to the Indians because of their black cassocks, described Kateri in their writings as a sensitive girl who wore a blanket over her head to hide her scarred face. After converting to Catholicism, she took a personal vow of virginity, offering herself to Jesus as her only husband. While Kateri continued to carry her share of the workload for women in her longhouse, she also began to avoid social gatherings, attracting intensifying persecution from her adopted family members who accused her of sorcery for becoming Christian and refusing to marry.

Even though the Jesuit fathers tried to protect Kateri from these sufferings, she embraced the hardships, sleeping on thorns in her mat at night while praying for the conversion and forgiveness of her relatives. In words often quoted by hagiographers, Kateri declared:

> I am not my own; I have given myself to Jesus. He must be my only love. The state of helpless poverty that may befall me if I do not marry does not frighten me. All I need is a little food and a few pieces of clothing. With the work of my hands I shall always earn what is necessary and what is left over I'll give to my relatives and to the poor. If I should become sick and unable to work, then I shall be like the Lord on the cross. He will have mercy on me and help me, I am sure.

At age twenty, about a year after her baptism, Kateri fled her village and relocated to the Jesuit mission village of Kahnawake, south of Montreal in modern-day Canada. There she spent the last few years of her life in prayer and penance, ultimately dying in the arms of a fellow Indian maiden and dear friend with the words: "Jesus, Mary, I love you."

After Kateri's death, her reputation for holiness quickly spread, attracting pilgrims to her graveside to pray. To protect her grave from these crowds, the Jesuits turned her bones to dust and set the ashes within a newly rebuilt chapel next to it, symbolizing her presence and allowing visitors to pray with her relics for healing. In 2012, Pope Benedict XVI canonized her as St. Kateri Tekakwitha, "the lily of the Mohawks."

To have Jesuits working with such dedication among the Mohawk Indians, as they did with this young woman, was a dangerous ministry at that time. Only seven years before St. Kateri Tekakwitha was born, the last of several "Black Robe" martyrs was tomahawked to death by Indian braves in the area around Auriesville, New York. The most famous of these martyrs were Jean de Brébeuf and Isaac Jogues, and it is to their story I now turn.

The North American Martyrs

In the early 1600s, French Jesuits came by the boatload to New France, determined to learn the languages of the American Indians and spend the rest of their lives evangelizing natives like St. Kateri Tekakwitha. They left Europe fully expecting they would never return home or see their family and friends again; most of them didn't. St. Jean de Brébeuf and St. Isaac Jogues, two Jesuits working among Kateri's people, have come to be the best-known of the eight North American Martyrs we celebrate at Mass each year on October 19.

All eight of these martyrs were French Jesuits. Jean de Brébeuf (1593–1649), born in Normandy, entered the Jesuit novitiate in Rouen at age twenty-four after his university studies. He took vows following the customary two-year novitiate, taught young boys at the Jesuit school in Rouen for three years, and was finally ordained a priest in 1622.

The newly ordained Fr. Brébeuf became treasurer of the school in Rouen and continued to work there until 1625, when he left as a volunteer for the Huron Indian mission of New France, located more than nine hundred miles from Quebec. A tall and imposing thirty-two-year-old with the strength of an ox, he seemed well-suited for the job.

Attaching himself with two other priests to a Huron trading party that came to barter at the French Canadian settlements, Fr. Brébeuf traveled for thirty days — mostly over water and by canoe, but carrying the boats overland when necessary — to Huronia. His Huron guides called the huge French priest "Echon" ("man-who-carries-the-load") because of his strength.

For two years, he studied Huron language, customs, and beliefs among the Bear Clan, writing a Huron grammar and phrase book in addition to translating a catechism. However, converts were rare and many natives blamed Brébeuf for bad weather (always a threat to their crops and lives) until on one occasion he was able to make a show of dispelling it with his prayers. After this initial preparation, he spent two more years preaching the Gospel, visiting the sick in their homes, and baptizing the dying, but still he made no healthy adult converts.

In 1629, the French surrendered to the English at Quebec, driving all of their citizens and missionaries out of the region. Fr. Brébeuf was forced to return to France, becoming chaplain at Rouen and treasurer of the college at Eu. But three years later, Quebec came back into French hands, and he returned to the Huron mission in 1633. For Brébeuf, his commitment to the Huron people was not a temporary thing to be abandoned in the face of obstacles.

The Death of Father Brébeuf

From 1633 to 1640, Fr. Brébeuf established a growing network of Jesuit missions among the Huron villages and was joined by new Jesuit recruits who helped teach Catholicism to Indians in their cabins and baptize the dying. During small-pox epidemics and droughts, these baptisms elicited suspicion from Huron magicians who observed that their people always died after the sacrament and who blamed the cross above the Jesuit cabins for lack of rain. In 1640, a Huron council finally decided Fr. Brébeuf and the other Black Robes had to die, obliging him to move between the villages and Quebec more frequently to avoid endangering the mission.

Throughout these years, despite the low number of con-verts, the Jesuit missionaries to modern-day Canada and up-state New York recorded their experiences of the exotic Ameri-can Indian culture in letters to their superiors in France. These reports from remote Jesuit mission outposts, published back home in an annual collection called *The Jesuit Relations and Allied Documents,* created a sensation among French Catholics who soon clamored to join the Society of Jesus or at least go to New France as lay assistants in the Jesuit missions. Many of these zealous recruits were inflamed by the ideal of dedicating their lives out of love to bring the natives to Christianity, dy-ing a martyr's death if necessary.

In one letter published in *The Jesuit Relations,* now read at the Liturgy of the Hours as the second reading for Matins on the October 19 feast of the North American Martyrs, St. Jean de Brébeuf wrote movingly of his own desire for martyr-dom as he realized his days were increasingly numbered:

> For two days now I have experienced a great desire to be a martyr and to endure all the torments the martyrs suffered.
>
> Jesus, my Lord and my Savior, what can I give you in return for all the favors you have conferred on me? I will take from your hand the cup of your sufferings and call on your name. I vow before your

eternal Father and the Holy Spirit, before your most
holy Mother and her most chaste spouse, before
the angels, apostles, and martyrs, before my most
blessed fathers St. Ignatius and St. Francis Xavier —
in truth I vow to you, Jesus my Savior, that as far as
I have strength I will never fail to accept the grace of
martyrdom, if some day you in your infinite mercy
should offer it to me, your most unworthy servant.

I bind myself in this way so that for the rest
of my life I will have neither permission nor freedom to refuse opportunities of dying and shedding
my blood for you, unless at a particular juncture I
should consider it more suitable for your glory to
act otherwise at that time. Further, I bind myself to
this so that on receiving the blow of death, I shall
accept it from your hands with the fullest delight
and joy of spirit. For this reason, my beloved Jesus,
and because of the surging joy which moves me,
here and now I offer my blood and body and life.
May I die only for you, if you will grant me this
grace, since you willingly died for me. Let me so
live so that you may grant me the gift of such a
happy death. In this way, my God and Savior, I will
take from your hand the cup of your sufferings and
call on your name: Jesus, Jesus, Jesus!

My God, it grieves me greatly that you are not
known, that in this savage wilderness all have not
been converted to you, that sin has not been driv-
en from it. My God, even if all the brutal tortures
which prisoners in this region must endure should
fall on me, I offer myself most willingly to them
and I alone shall suffer them all.

Fr. Brébeuf packs a lot of Ignatian spirituality into this letter, from his personal vow to accept martyrdom for Christ in language that recalls the Jesuit vow formula ("before your eternal Father" and "before your most holy Mother") to the self-offering ("I offer myself") that recalls the *Suscipe* ("Receive") prayer of St. Ignatius of Loyola.

The *Suscipe*, prayed by every Jesuit from Fr. Brébeuf to Pope Francis, is an act of total self-dedication of one's life to God. There are many English translations of it floating around, but I prefer to use my own version:

Receive, Lord, all my liberty.
Take my memory, my understanding, and my entire will.
All that I have and possess, you have given to me.
To you, O Lord, I return it.
Dispose of it wholly according to your will.
Give me only your love and your grace
and I am rich enough and ask for nothing more. Amen.

For St. Jean de Brébeuf, this prayer was not an idea but a reality: He knew he was going to die, he had a good idea how he was going to die, and yet he chose to stay with his Huron Indians anyway. Like countless generations of Jesuits from St. Edmund Campion to Fr. Frans van der Lugt, he didn't want to die and did his best to avoid it. But he also prayed for the grace to desire martyrdom if it came as an unavoidable consequence of his commitment to the Huron people.

As the Huron Indians declined due to illness and became Christianized, the Iroquois and other tribes seized on this perceived weakness to invade several of their villages, killing the Jesuit missionaries along with the Huron natives. St. Isaac Jogues was martyred in October 1646 and St. Anthony Daniel in July 1648. Finally, Iroquois warriors destroyed the Saint-Ignace and Saint-Louis villages in 1649, capturing St. Gabriel Lallemant and St. Jean de Brébeuf at the latter.

When the Iroquois learned they had captured the chief Jesuit "sorcerer," they slaughtered the sick and elderly Huron villagers in Saint-Louis, setting it on fire. Then they stripped and tortured the Christian missionaries, led them naked through the winter snows back to Saint-Ignace, and forced the priests to run the gauntlet there.

At the end, Fr. Lallemant and Fr. Brébeuf were tied to two poles and systematically butchered by the Iroquois braves, who inflicted tortures on every part of their bodies. But they were unable to intimidate the fearless Fr. Brébeuf, whose silence toward them and exhortations to his fellow prisoners throughout the tortures enraged them. In a hysterical frenzy, the Iroquois finally removed the heart of this gentle giant and ate it in an effort to steal his courage. In this way, St. Jean de Brébeuf, Apostle to the Hurons, died at the age of forty-six on the afternoon of March 16, 1649, after twenty years on the North American missions. The Jesuits recovered his body and the remains of St. Gabriel Lallemant, who had only joined the missions one year earlier, and buried them.

St. Isaac Jogues

Before concluding this chapter, I want to say a word about another one of the eight North American Martyrs, St. Isaac Jogues. As I mentioned above, he was martyred three years before St. Jean de Brébeuf. But there is one detail that makes this saint stand out from the rest: Fr. Jogues died after being captured, tortured, escaping, and *choosing to return* to the Indians who had disfigured him.

As a seventeen-year-old boy in Orléans, France, St. Isaac Jogues (1607–1646) had entered the Jesuits after being inspired to become a missionary by reading *The Jesuit Relations*. Following his novitiate at Rouen, philosophy studies at La Fleche, and theology studies at Clermont College in Paris, he was ordained a priest in January 1636 and left shortly afterward for the missions in New France.

Assigned to the Huron mission, Fr. Jogues earned the nickname "Ondessonk" (Bird of Prey) from the Indians, who could not pronounce his name. Meeting his hero Fr. Brébeuf in Huronia, he quickly mastered the Huron language and began instructing the natives in Catholicism. After evangelizing the Hurons at Sainte-Marie, where a visiting delegation of Chippewas asked the Black Robes to establish a similar mission among their villages, he began making plans to take his converts to evangelize the western tribes.

Eager to reach out to these tribes, Fr. Jogues explored the edges of Huron territory with St. René Goupil, a surgeon he had recruited in Quebec as a lay assistant to the Jesuit missionaries. These trips placed him in increasing danger.

In August 1642, a war party of seventy Mohawk braves descended on a flotilla of Huron boats carrying Jogues and Goupil, forcing them to land. As the Mohawks assaulted the Christian party on shore, Fr. Jogues began to flee into the woods, only to stop suddenly at the thought of his Hurons being deprived of a priest in captivity. Turning around, he walked calmly back to the shore and surrendered himself to the terrified Mohawk braves, who could not believe he had returned.

Singling out the Frenchmen, the Mohawks beat and mutilated Goupil and Jogues, bringing them deep into their territory to Ossernenon, the future birthplace of St. Kateri Tekakwitha. As the war party took them along the rivers and paths to this village, Goupil expressed his desire to become a Jesuit brother on the spot, and professed his perpetual vows of poverty, chastity, and obedience to Fr. Jogues.

Stripped and tortured by Mohawk villagers along the way, the two Jesuits ran the gauntlet in Ossernenon and were tied to poles where the village warriors stabbed them. The Mohawks removed the left thumb and index finger of Fr. Jogues, disfiguring those digits on his right hand as well. Then they confined the two Jesuits to a longhouse where children tortured them with hot coals. The chief who captured them made them his personal slaves.

One sunny day a few weeks after arriving at this village, Br. Goupil was playing with some of the Indian children, teaching them how to make the Sign of the Cross. Some of the village braves, witnessing this action, grew angry at the sight and dragged him into the woods with Fr. Jogues following. There they hacked Goupil to death with a tomahawk.

Fr. Jogues, rushing up to the body of St. René Goupil, said the necessary prayers over it and extended his neck to await his own death blow. But the Mohawks walked away, leaving him to bury the body of Br. Goupil in a makeshift Christian grave. Isaac Jogues was all alone now.

The Escape and Return of Father Jogues

For several months, Fr. Jogues labored as a slave while quietly serving as priest for the Christian Hurons who had been captured with him, occasionally sneaking off into the woods to pray to God at a makeshift cross he had constructed with branches.

But during a September 1643 trading trip to the Dutch settlement of Fort Orange in modern-day Albany, New York, some sympathetic Dutchmen hid him in one of their ships for six weeks and waited until his Mohawk captors stopped looking for him. In November, the Dutch then shipped Fr. Jogues to England, where he worked his way across the channel to Brittany. Coming ashore in France for the first time in seven years, he attended Mass and confession at a peasant church before reporting to the nearest Jesuit community in Rennes, which received him as a martyr returned from the dead.

Unable to celebrate Mass properly because of his disfigured hands, Fr. Jogues obtained a dispensation from Pope Urban

XIII, who told the Jesuits: "It would be shameful that a martyr of Christ be not allowed to drink the blood of Christ."

After visiting his mother at Orléans in April 1644, Fr. Jogues returned to the North American missions, attending the Three Rivers peace conference between the Iroqouis and French in the summer. Selected as an envoy to obtain Mohawk consent for the peace treaty before it could be ratified, he departed with two Algonquins and four Mohawks for the village of his enslavement in May 1646.

Shortly before leaving for Ossernenon, as he waited for word on whether he would in fact go at all, Fr. Jogues told a Jesuit friend in a letter that he did not expect to return from such a trip. Yet despite his conviction of certain death, this "Letter to a Friend" captures the saint's resolve to return to the Mohawk people even if it became his last journey:

> The Iroquois have come to make some presents to our governor, ransom some prisoners he held, and treat of peace with him in the name of the whole country. It has been concluded, to the great joy of France. It will last as long as pleases the Almighty.
>
> To maintain, and see what can be done for the instruction of these tribes, it is here deemed expedient to send them some father. I have reason to think I shall be sent, since I have some knowledge of the language and country. You see what need I have of the powerful aid of prayers while amidst these savages. I will have to remain among them, almost without liberty to pray, without Mass, without Sacraments, and be responsible for every accident among the Iroquois, French, Algonquins, and others.
>
> But what shall I say? My hope is in God, who needs not us to accomplish his designs. We must

endeavor to be faithful to Him and not spoil His work by our shortcomings....

My heart tells me that if I have the happiness of being employed in this mission, *Ibo et non redibo* (I shall go and shall not return); but I shall be happy if our Lord will complete the sacrifice where He has begun it, and make the little blood I have shed in that land the earnest of what I would give from every vein of my body and my heart.

In a word, this people is "a bloody spouse" to me (Exodus 4:25). May our good Master, who has purchased them in His blood, open to them the door of His Gospel, as well as to the four allied nations near them.

Adieu, dear Father. Pray Him to unite me inseparably to Him.

Isaac Jogues, S.J.

Farewell, he writes, adding: I go, but I shall not return. Not long after this letter, Fr. Jogues grew tired of waiting and asked his superior directly for permission to go south from Quebec back to Ossernenon. His request was granted. Many Jesuits, including me, might have done everything possible to *excuse* ourselves from this assignment. But St. Isaac Jogues said *yes*, as he was not a man to put limits on his commitment. And so he returned with a peace treaty to the Indians who had tortured, enslaved, and humiliated him.

The Martyrdom of Isaac Jogues

Fr. Jogues led a band of Hurons and a Jesuit brother, the experienced woodsman St. John de la Lande, back toward the village where St. René Goupil still lay in the ground — but their diplomatic mission, unknown to them, was doomed from the start. Not far into their journey, they learned that the Mohawks were on the warpath, and all but one of their Huron guides fled back to Three Rivers. As the two missionaries and their remaining Huron ally paddled along the river, the Mohawks at Ossernenon were already working themselves into a fury against Jogues, blaming his chest of Catholic liturgical items for causing failed crops and an epidemic.

So it unfolded that a Mohawk death squad, taking to the waterways on a mission to kill any Frenchmen they found, stumbled across the hated Fr. Jogues and his party on the river not far from their village on October 17. Stripping and beating them, the Mohawks carried the three men back to Ossernenon, torturing them before a crowd of villagers.

On October 18, as St. Isaac Jogues was recovering from these latest tortures, an Indian brave invited him to a feast at the chief's lodge. But as Fr. Jogues entered the lodge, he was ambushed by another Mohawk hiding inside the entrance. In an instant, this brave crushed the priest's skull with a tomahawk, dragging his body through the village. That evening, when Br. de la Lande stuck his head out of his lodge in the hope of sneaking off to recover the body, a brave waiting outside the entrance did the same thing to him.

On the Reservation

We Jesuits have a long history of missionary work with native peoples, some of it successful and some of it not so glorious. While the Spanish and Portuguese Jesuit missions in seventeenth-century South America thrived and prospered, with martyrs like St. Roque Gonzalez (1576-1628) planting seeds that grew into today's large Catholic population on that continent, the French Jesuit missions in North America during the same period ended in illness and decline. Yet in spite of this reality, which came about partly because Latin American tribes intermarried with European colonists while North

American tribes did not, we Jesuits have continued to operate North American Indian missions to this very day.

In the Midwestern and Western United States, the Jesuit Fathers Jacques Marquette (1637–1675) and Servant of God Eusebio Kino (1645–1711) were more successful at earning the trust of North American Indians than the early martyrs. Building on their progress, in the nineteenth century, Jesuit Fr. Pierre-Jean de Smet (1801–1873) finally accepted an invitation from the Flathead Indians in Idaho to travel to the northern plains, where the Jesuits established missions just as the U.S. government began to conquer and resettle the last free Indian nations.

Forced to resettle their Lakota Sioux nations on reservations in South Dakota, Chief Spotted Tail of Rosebud Reservation and Chief Red Cloud of Pine Ridge Reservation later met with U.S. President Rutherford B. Hayes to formally request that the Black Robes (as distinct from the shirt-wearers, i.e., Protestant ministers) be assigned to establish the Christian missions on their lands. Chief Red Cloud told President Hayes that the Black Robes ran schools that he saw as essential to the survival of his people:

> I would like to say something about a teacher. My children, all of them, would like to learn how to talk English. They would like to learn how to read and write. We have teachers there, but all they teach us is to talk Sioux, and to write Sioux, and that is not necessary. I would like to get Catholic priests. Those who wear black dresses. These men will teach us how to read and write English.

The Jesuits who first came to these two reservations established a school on each of them in addition to a network of thirty-seven mission stations. Since that time, many of these stations have closed, and the Jesuits turned over the St. Francis

School at Rosebud to the tribe in 1974. But we continue to
minister among the Lakota Sioux as guests on their land.
In June 2013, I led a group of students from Jesuit High
School of Tampa to the St. Francis Mission on the Rosebud
Indian Reservation, where we Jesuits operate a radio station and
six parishes in addition to a drug addiction rehabilitation center.
Not just anyone can enter an Indian reservation. Driving
onto Rosebud in our rental van as guests of the Jesuit mission,
we felt like we were entering "international waters" as we listened to drumbeats and Indian pow-wow chants on the reservation radio station. Legally, American Indian reservations are
semi-sovereign territories directly subject to federal jurisdiction;
they are not formally part of the United States or of the states
in which they reside. That means state laws do not apply on
reservation lands, and the tribe, not the governor, has police
jurisdiction over everything short of a federal offense.

This system has unintentionally turned the reservations
into hotbeds of illiteracy, alcoholism, and other human mis-
eries. The Sicangu Lakota Sioux represent a defeated people,
living in government housing on arid land given to them by
the U.S. government as compensation for stealing their fertile
land. Jesuits, who represent Christianity there, also represent
the conquering palefaces.

One experiences America differently on a reservation.
On June 25, we danced in a tribal pow-wow to celebrate the
anniversary of the death of General George Armstrong Custer.
Fr. John Hatcher, S.J., superior of the Jesuit mission, led a
prayer in the Lakota Sioux language at this pow-wow. Then
on July 4, we celebrated Independence Day at the home of
a Catholic Sioux family from the Jesuit mission, lighting off
enormous fireworks which would be illegal anywhere else
within the continental United States.

When our students asked about the history of the Jesuit missions in North America, I referred them to the Bruce

Beresford film *Black Robe*, from 1991, but cautioned them that it was rated "R" for sex and violence. One kid, amazed, asked me how a film about priests could be rated "R." At a loss for where to begin, I simply smiled and shrugged.

There are no corporations, name-brand stores, gas stations, or restaurant chains on an Indian reservation, but there are often Indian casinos nearby. Throughout our two-week trip, we slept in the youth center at a Jesuit parish and bought food at the reservation store to cook dinner. But our high school boys inhaled fast food whenever we traveled off the reservation to get gasoline, tour buffalo preserves, or visit "the faces" (an Indian nickname) of Mt. Rushmore. Meanwhile, we worked daily with Indian children and the lay members of the Jesuit Volunteer Corps in a Bible summer camp.

We also attended a sun dance, a sacred Indian ritual that feels like something from the seventeenth century, but we could not take photos or video, and we were asked not to share what we experienced with anyone. (It is rare for outsiders to be invited at all, but we were allowed to attend because of the Jesuit connection.)

Some hostilities and resentments continue to linger among Indians who don't want the Jesuits or any other outsiders on their lands: We saw anti-Christian graffiti on some mission buildings. Yet the Jesuits on these reservations, mirroring the attitude of Jesuits on our Inuit Indian missions in Alaska, have committed themselves to stay with the Lakota Sioux as long as possible. These lands with their broken people are part of the "margins" Pope Francis calls us to embrace.

We Jesuits may not have earned a place at the lodge in these Indian territories, but we've certainly worked — and bled — for it.

CHAPTER SEVEN

GRATITUDE

*If today a man may hear Mass in Warsaw or hope that
the classics shall survive our modern decay, he owes it to
the Society of Jesus.*

— Hilaire Belloc, *How the Reformation Happened*

In France, a twenty-three-year-old woman named Margaret returned home in an expensive dress from a Carnival ball one night to experience, in prayer, a vision of the scourged and bloody Jesus. This image of Jesus chastised Margaret for neglecting him but added that his heart was full of love for her.

A quiet and pious Burgundian, Margaret Alacoque had spent much of her sickly childhood praying in front of the Blessed Sacrament after her dad died when she was eight, plunging the family into poverty. When she was seventeen, her family recovered its wealth and her mother started sending Margaret to society balls to find a husband. Yet she retained her piety.

The deeply religious Margaret took her Mardi Gras vision of Jesus seriously and decided, shortly before her twenty-fourth birthday, to fulfill a childhood vow by entering the Visitation Convent at Paray-le-Monial as a cloistered nun. Entering the convent, she added the religious name Mary to her baptismal name.

St. Margaret Mary Alacoque (1647–1690), as we know her today, struggled in religious life as she continued to have visions of Jesus showing his heart to her and calling her the "Beloved Disciple of the Sacred Heart." She claimed Jesus asked her to establish an annual feast of the Sacred Heart on the Friday after Corpus Christi. But her religious superiors, thinking her delusional, discouraged her from paying attention to these visions.

Catholics, of course, are never bound to believe in the private revelations that individuals experience in prayer, as we have the public revelation of Jesus Christ in Scripture and Tradition to supply the fundamentals of our faith. Yet Sr. Margaret Mary, who eventually became novice mistress, faced a great deal of hostility from her religious sisters. And she still managed to see a convent chapel built to the Sacred Heart before she died of an illness at the age of forty-three.

Giving a hint of her contemplative prayer life, St. Margaret Mary Alacoque wrote the following in her journal:

> We should always look to God as in ourselves, no matter in what manner we meditate upon Him, so as to accustom ourselves to dwell in His divine presence. For when we behold Him within our souls, all our powers and faculties, and even our senses, are recollected within us. If we look at God apart from ourselves we are easily distracted by exterior objects.

In time, Sr. Margaret Mary convinced the mother superior her visions were authentic, but she failed to persuade a group of theologians to endorse them. It was only when a young Jesuit priest came to the Visitation Convent as spiritual director and confessor to the nuns that she gained the support she needed to share her visions publicly. Today we know this young Jesuit as St. Claude La Colombière.

St. Claude La Colombière

While many Jesuits have been intellectuals and academics, St. Claude La Colombière (1641–1682) was a man of the heart, making him the perfect spiritual guide for St. Margaret Mary Alacoque. Because he was a sensitive and deeply prayerful man, his Jesuit spirituality allowed him to grasp the depth of Margaret's visions where others did not. But Fr. Colombière also suffered deeply, dying at forty-one, several years before Sr. Margaret Mary passed away and before her chapel was completed, and his time at the Visitation convent proved to be brief.

Born in southern France, young Claude studied grammar and philosophy at the Jesuit school in Lyons, where he admired his Jesuit teachers and decided to enter the Society in 1658 when he was seventeen. Following his vows and philosophy studies, he taught grammar and literature at Trinity College in Avignon from 1661 to 1666 and completed his theology studies at the College of Clermont in Paris. Upon being ordained a priest in 1670 at the age of twenty-nine, Fr. Claude taught rhetoric at Lyons, and after three years he became preacher at the parish attached to the school.

After ordination, Fr. Claude also became superior of a small Jesuit house in Paray-le-Monial, meeting Sr. Margaret Mary on his first visit to the nearby convent. Precisely at the moment when she felt most misunderstood by her fellow sisters, he became her spiritual director.

One hallmark of Ignatian spirituality, exemplified by Fr. Claude as much as by St. Alphonsus Rodriguez and Pope Francis, is the gift of "spiritual conversation." In spiritual direction, we Jesuits are trained to always take a person's religious experiences seriously, creating a space to contemplate what God is doing in a person's life and to talk about it more deeply. That is precisely what St. Claude La Colombière did with St. Margaret Mary, who opened her inner life to him completely and shared supernatural experiences that moved him deeply.

The focus in spiritual direction, for a Jesuit like St. Claude, will always be on what God is doing rather than on what the directee or director is doing. What does the person want from God and where is God present in his or her life? How is the person bringing his or her desires to God in prayer, and how is God responding? What does he or she notice about God's response?

In his prayer Center of Our Hearts, St. Claude La Colombière articulates this interior centering of one's heart on Jesus Christ that remains a distinguishing feature of Ignatian spirituality from St. Ignatius to Pope Francis:

O God, what will you do to conquer
the fearful hardness of our hearts?
Lord, you must give us new hearts,
tender hearts, sensitive hearts,
to replace hearts that are made of marble and of bronze.

You must give us your own Heart, Jesus.
Come, lovable Heart of Jesus.
Place your Heart deep in the center of our hearts
and enkindle in each heart a flame of love
as strong, as great, as the sum of all the reasons
that I have for loving you, my God.

O holy Heart of Jesus, dwell hidden in my heart,
so that I may live only in you and only for you,
so that, in the end, I may live with you eternally in heaven.
Amen.

We see here that the direction of this prayer is vertical, not horizontal; it is a person's conversation *with* the Lord rather than a person talking *about* the Lord to himself or to someone else. It is the prayer of a person *inviting* the Lord into his heart as the main focus of his consideration, rather than a person *talking about* and *thinking about* his problems to himself with the illusion that he is somehow praying. St. Claude's prayer illustrates how Ignatian spirituality emphasizes the relationship we have with Jesus above all else; it is about savoring and giving thanks for the graces the Lord gives us in prayer rather than *talking at* him.

For a Jesuit, any kind of spiritual direction that consists of a director teaching religion to someone, or giving advice to a person about life's problems, is really pastoral counseling rather than spiritual direction, because the point of the latter is to talk about *our relationship with Jesus Christ in prayer* and not exclusively about ourselves as in psychotherapy. Although even many good Catholics may have trouble believing Jesus speaks to them directly in prayer, a good Ignatian spiritual director like St. Claude — whether lay, Jesuit, or from another religious order — will be trained to help us trust and deepen our religious experiences in conversation. Our thankful experience of God's words and deeds in prayer, far from being a delusion or distraction, should always be the central image of any Ignatian spiritual conversation.

The Suffering and Death of St. Claude

As their conversations about Sr. Margaret Mary's experiences of the Sacred Heart of Jesus developed, Fr. Claude discerned with deep gratitude that God was indeed speaking to her authentically. But he only stayed in Paray-le-Monial for eighteen months before his superiors assigned him to become preacher to the Duchess of York in London. King Charles II had given permission for the duchess and her husband to have a Catholic chapel in St. James Palace, despite the the contunuing persecution of Catholics in England.

In his sermons to the duke and duchess of York after arriving at the palace in October 1676, Fr. Claude preached the love of Jesus for all people, developing the image of the Sacred Heart, pierced by a lance on the cross, pouring out the Lord's love in blood and water. (For many years these sermons stayed with the duchess, who later became the first royal person to ask Pope Innocent XII to establish a feast of the Sacred Heart.) In the second reading for Matins on his feast day, provided in

the Supplement to the Divine Office for the Society of Jesus,
we read this excerpt from St. Claude's spiritual notes that he
wrote from London in 1677:

> My God, if only I could travel all over the world
> and proclaim in every country what you require of
> your servants and friends! When God revealed his
> will to this person [St. Margaret Mary Alacoque],
> and she had communicated it to me, I told her to
> put it down in writing. I have no scruples about
> copying the words into my retreat journal, for it
> is God's will to use me in this cause. These are the
> holy woman's words:
>
> "Being in the presence of the Blessed Sacra-
> ment one day of the octave [of Corpus Christi], I
> received from God excessive graces of His love. I
> was moved by the desire of making some return and
> of giving love for love, and He told me: 'You could
> not make me a greater return than to do what I
> have so often asked of you.'
>
> "And showing me His divine heart: 'Behold
> the heart which has loved men so much that it has
> spared nothing, even to exhausting and consuming
> itself, to prove its love to them. And as thanks I
> receive from the greater number only ingratitude,
> because of the disregard, the irreverence, the sac-
> rilege, and the coldness which they have for Me in
> this sacrament of love. But what is still more offen-
> sive is that these are hearts which are consecrated to
> me. That is why I ask that the first Friday after the
> octave of Corpus Christi be dedicated as a special
> feast to honor My heart by making a reparation of
> honor, by an *amende honorable*, by receiving Com-
> munion on that day to repair the indignities which

it has suffered during the hours it was exposed on the altars. And I promise that My heart will expand to pour out with abundance the graces of its divine love on those who will render it this honor.'

"'But, dear Lord [she answered], to whom are you applying? To a wretched creature, a poor sinner whose very unworthiness would be capable even of preventing the accomplishment of Your plan? You have so many generous souls to carry out your purpose.'

"'Ah, poor innocent that you are [Christ replied], don't you know that I make use of the weakest subjects to confound the strong, that it is ordinarily the smallest and the poor in spirit to whom I make my power visible with greater brilliance, so that they will not attribute anything to themselves?'

"'Give me, then,' I said to Him, 'the means of doing what you command.'

"It was then that He told me: 'Turn to my servant [Claude La Colombière] and tell him from Me to do all he can to establish this devotion and to give this pleasure to My divine heart. Tell him not to be discouraged by the difficulties he will meet with, for they will not be lacking. But he must learn that he is all-powerful who completely distrusts himself to place his trust in Me alone.'"

Like the Sacred Heart he promoted as a way of growing closer to Jesus in gratitude, giving to others out of love for the Lord who first loved him, St. Claude spent himself in service quickly, and his assignment in London again proved brief. Denounced as a traitor by false witnesses eager to receive the reward of one hundred pounds promised by the government for informing on a Jesuit, Fr. Colombière was arrested early one morning in November 1678 and thrown into a cold dungeon until December. When the sensitive preacher suffered a series of hemorrhages in this dungeon, the government simply released and deported him, reasoning he was no real threat as a non-Englishman and would be better off in his own country.

Back in Paris by mid-January 1679, the battered priest made his way to Lyons, where his broken health limited him to serving as spiritual director for the Jesuit seminarians at Trinity College beginning in March. Even as his health worsened, St. Claude continued with greater fervor than ever to preach the love of Jesus in the Sacred Heart.

In August 1681, Fr. Colombière returned to his beloved Paray-le-Monial to recover his health, being so weak at this point that he needed help dressing and undressing. Early in February 1682, he caught a fever and lingered in it for several days, finally dying with words of thanks on his lips for the love of Jesus. He was buried in this town where his grave remains today, and we Jesuits celebrate his feast on February 15, the day he died.

Devotion to the Sacred Heart

After St. Claude La Colombière passed away, succeeding generations of Jesuits continued to spread devotion to the Sacred Heart of Jesus, preaching the visions of St. Margaret Mary, until Pope Pius IX finally established a universal feast of the Sacred Heart of Jesus in 1856. A group of French Jesuits had already created the Apostleship of Prayer in 1844, encouraging its members to offer each day to God in union with the Sacred Heart.

In the late 1800s, the pope began issuing monthly prayer intentions through the Apostleship of Prayer, which asked its members to pray for them daily. Today, Pope Francis continues the tradition of declaring two prayer intentions for each month, and members of the Apostleship of Prayer — which is now officially known as "The Pope's Worldwide Prayer Network (Apostleship of Prayer)" and is a pontifical mission entrusted to the Society of Jesus — commit to pray for them. Members may also consecrate themselves to the Sacred Heart of Jesus and wear the Sacred Heart badge. But the Daily Offering (also called the Morning Offering) prayer, which one can recite anywhere and anytime, remains the only requirement of membership. A new version of the Daily Offering, approved by the Jesuit general a few years ago, reads as follows:

> God, our Father, I offer you my day. I offer you my prayers, thoughts, words, actions, joys, and sufferings in union with the Heart of Jesus, who continues to offer Himself in the Eucharist for the salvation of the world. May the Holy Spirit, who guided Jesus, be my guide and my strength today so that I may witness to your love. With Mary, the mother of our Lord and the Church, I pray for all Apostles of Prayer and for the prayer intentions proposed by the Holy Father this month. Amen.

As a young girl in France, St. Thérèse of Lisieux (1873–1897) was enrolled in the Apostleship of Prayer, experiencing great devotion in uniting her prayers to the Sacred Heart. The Daily Offering that she and many others have practiced remains an easy devotion that we can fit into our busy lives even today, with or without knowing the precise monthly intentions of the pope. It's a small way of turning our hearts to Jesus in the midst of our busy lives.

For some Catholics today, the Sacred Heart may feel a bit strange, as the various images of Jesus holding his inflamed heart in front of his body and pointing to it may recall a by-

gone spirituality. Yet the vision of Christ's opened heart, a symbol of his love for each and every one of us, conveys a sense of
love that inspires many people to gratitude for the gifts we've
received from God. In praying with a statue or painting of the
Sacred Heart, we may find ourselves contemplating all that Jesus went through for us, reflecting with thanksgiving on God
giving himself to us in his suffering and death. And as we pray
the Daily Offering, or simply pray "O Most Sacred Heart of
Jesus, have mercy on me," we can taste and savor each word as
a gift from the Lord, reflecting on the same heart poured out
in love that St. Margaret Mary told St. Claude about in their
conversations.

Saintly Scholars

But not all Jesuits have lived as great missionaries or spiritual
directors. Many Jesuit saints have instead distinguished themselves as great academics and scholars, including two of the
thirty-six people recognized as Doctors of the Church for their
contributions to theology and doctrine. Before I conclude this
chapter, I want to talk about these two Jesuit doctors: St. Peter
Canisius, an early recruit to the Society who continued the
work of St. Peter Faber in Germany, and the great cardinal-
theologian St. Robert Bellarmine.

During his fifty-four years in the Society of Jesus, St. Peter
Canisius (1521–1597) founded eighteen colleges and wrote
thirty-seven books, but it was his preaching in German-speak-
ing countries that gave him fame as a leader of the Counter-
Reformation. Known as the "second apostle of Germany," sec-
ond only to the eighth-century Benedictine missionary-monk
St. Boniface, Fr. Canisius did not merely admit St. Stanislaus
Kostka into the Jesuit novitiate, but prevented the wavering
Catholic strongholds in Germany and Switzerland (as well as
Austria) from turning Protestant. His apologetics, or writings

and sermons in defense of the faith, earned him the title Doctor of the Church when Pope Pius XI canonized him in 1925.

He was born Peter Kanis, later Latinizing his name to "Canisius," in the town of Nijmegen in the Netherlands. A brilliant scholar, the young Dutchman left his homeland at age fourteen for Germany, where he completed a master's degree at the University of Cologne in May 1540, when he was only nineteen. This same year, the Society of Jesus was founded, and the new order soon came to the attention of the young Canisius, who was considering the priesthood. He traveled to Mainz to meet St. Peter Faber, the deeply spiritual co-founder of the order, who had once roomed with St. Ignatius and St. Francis Xavier at the University of Paris.

Fr. Faber, impressed by the young man's learning, led Canisius in the Spiritual Exercises. During the second week of this retreat, Canisius decided to enter the new order. So Fr. Faber received Canisius as a novice on his twenty-second birthday, May 8, 1543.

Due to his impressive educational background, his formation for the priesthood advanced rapidly. Canisius spent much of the time teaching Scripture and publishing new editions of St. Cyril of Alexandria and St. Leo the Great — and soon he returned to Cologne to finish his theology studies. After only three years in the Society, he was ordained a priest at the age of twenty-five on June 12, 1546.

From February to June 1547, the young Fr. Canisius served as a theological consultant for Cardinal Otto Truchsess at the Council of Trent, replacing his mentor Fr. Faber, who had died at Rome in August 1546 while preparing to attend the council. St. Ignatius then assigned him to teach at the Society's first school in Messina, Sicily, for two years. Impressed by the young priest's learning and ability to reach ordinary people, as well as by his administrative talents, Pope Paul III asked Fr. Canisius to return to Germany in September 1549

and defend the Catholic Church there from the Lutheran reformers by strengthening wavering Catholics and bringing
back lost sheep.

In hagiographical literature, one often finds saints coming up in the prayer of other saints, and Jesuits are no excep-
tion. As he prepared to leave Rome for Germany, Fr. Canisius
wrote the following words in his journal, recording an experience of gratitude to Christ's pierced heart and hope for his
German mission. We find this English translation of the text
in the second reading of Matins in the Divine Office for the
feast day of St. Peter Canisius, which the Society of Jesus celebrates in our houses on April 27 and the universal church
commemorates on December 21:

> Before he set out for Germany — he is rightly called
> the second apostle of that country — Saint Peter
> Canisius received the apostolic blessing, and under-
> went a profound spiritual experience. He describes
> it in these words.
>
> "Eternal High Priest, you allowed me in your
> boundless goodness to commend the fruit and con-
> firmation of that blessing to your apostles, to whom
> men go on pilgrimage to the Vatican and who there
> work wonders under your guidance. It was there
> that I experienced great consolation and the pres-
> ence of your grace, offered to me through these
> great intercessors. They too gave their blessings, and
> confirmed the mission to Germany; they seemed to
> promise their good will to me as an apostle of that
> country. You know, Lord, how strongly and how
> often you committed Germany to my care on that
> very day: I was to continue to be solicitous for it
> thereafter, I was to desire to live and die for it.

"At length, it was as if you opened to me the heart in your most sacred body: I seemed to see it directly before my eyes. You told me to drink from this fountain, inviting me, that is, to draw the waters of my salvation from your wellsprings, my Savior. I was most eager that streams of faith, hope, and love should flow into me from that source. I was thirsting for poverty, chastity, obedience. I asked to be made wholly clean by you, to be clothed by you, to be made resplendent by you.

"So, after daring to approach your most loving heart and to plunge my thirst in it, I received a promise from you of a garment made of three parts: these were to cover my soul in its nakedness, and to belong especially to my religious profession. They were peace, love, and perseverance. Protected by this garment of salvation, I was confident that I would lack nothing but all would succeed and give you glory."

This deep and thankful trust in God's providence would soon be tested. Canisius and a small group of the Society's priests arrived in November 1549 in Ingolstadt, Germany, and promptly secured teaching positions at the university. They found the religious situation there to be worse than expected: The University of Ingolstadt, nominally Catholic, found itself in a state of chaos wherein most students and faculty hadn't practiced their faith for many years.

In a letter to Fr. General Ignatius's personal secretary, dated roughly four months after his arrival, Fr. Canisius wrote that Catholicism was barely treading water in Ingolstadt and that he did not think he could get the university students to come to daily Mass even if he bribed them:

First of all, we have to be most careful in our lectures not to cite scholastic authorities often, nor to give allegorical interpretations of Scripture, if we wish to retain our present audience of students. They are beginning to fall away already, though we try our best to please them by avoiding too much subtlety and neglecting no part of duty. Would that there were even four or five of them whom we might hope to benefit by our lectures! As for the majority ... I certainly think no harm would be done by putting them back into the classes of grammar and rhetoric. In this university it is almost a convention that students need not trouble to study letters, least of all sacred letters....

Speaking generally, I may say that it is useless to look for practical interest in religion among present-day Germans. The divine worship of Catholics is reduced pretty well to the preaching of an uninspired sermon on feast-days. All that remains of the Lenten fast here is its name, for nobody fasts. And, oh, how rare it is for a man to visit a church, to go to Mass or to show by any outward sign that he still delights in the ancient faith. So much for the Catholics, or, rather, for those who keep the bare title of Catholic. At least one public Mass is said daily in our [Jesuit residence] chapel which is quite near to the students' living quarters and in the centre of the town. Yet, though two bells are rung to invite them, I do not believe that even were we to bribe them with gold we could induce a couple of these men to come to the Holy Sacrifice.

(Letter to Juan Polanco of March 24, 1550, as quoted on pp. 143–144 of *Saint Peter Canisius*, by Fr. James Brodrick, S.J., Jesuit Way reprint)

If one didn't know any better, one might think this letter was written by a Jesuit today, complaining about the things Jesuit university professors often gripe about: The students seem bored in class, they don't know how to read or write, they arrive unprepared to lectures, they have no genuine interest in religion, they ignore all the rules of the Church, they find the sermons by local priests uninspiring, and hardly any of them come to daily Mass. Faced with this situation at a school run by the Society today, some current Jesuits might react by complaining to their community at the nightly social before dinner. But Canisius, being a saint, chose to do something more constructive than play the blame game.

In prayer, Fr. Canisius discerned that the Catholic identity crisis of the university had one overriding cause: There was no educated person on hand who believed in Catholicism deeply enough to teach and explain the faith with conviction. Realizing it would be fruitless to spend his days hiding away comfortably in the Jesuit residence while lecturing occasionally to his bored university students, Fr. Canisius decided to go to the people himself, using his gift with words for popular defenses of the faith more than for academic research. Devoting all his time outside of academic duties to preaching, he ascended the pulpit to deliver a series of catechetical sermons on the fundamentals of Catholicism.

The Gratitude of St. Peter Canisius

During the three years he preached in Ingolstadt, Fr. Canisius saw Mass attendance rise significantly. His passion for the faith combined with his deep learning and ability to speak in ordinary language shocked people in the sleepy university town, as they had never encountered a priest who spoke so clearly and actually seemed to believe what he taught. His sermons became so popular that even Protestants attended them, some to learn about their powerful new enemy, and others simply to learn from him.

In February 1552, the Jesuits sent Canisius to the Austrian capital of Vienna to work his magic again. There he founded a seminary, recruited seminarians, and assumed the post of court preacher. Unfortunately, Canisius soon became so popular in his roles as preacher and administrator that a minor crisis arose when the pope and king tried to nominate him as the city's new bishop at age thirty-two, causing much anxiety to St. Ignatius back at Jesuit headquarters in Rome. But Fr. Canisius quietly ended this crisis with a compromise, agreeing to serve as diocesan administrator until a new bishop was appointed.

It was at Vienna that St. Peter Canisius wrote his first catechism, *Summary of Christian Doctrine*, which he published in April 1555. Using a simple question-and-answer format on a level intended for college students, the book spent more time on topics disputed by the Protestants and less time on topics of consensus. It became so popular that a German translation of the Latin original appeared in 1556, and versions for secondary school students (*Shorter Catechism*) and for young children in early religious education (*Catholic Catechism*) soon followed. These books went through two hundred printings in his lifetime and were reprinted continuously until the 1800s. (Not long ago, German Catholic parents still asked their children: "Do you know your Canisius?")

Leaving Vienna, Canisius opened a college at Prague in July 1555 and worked there until June 1556, when St. Ignatius of Loyola — in his last days as Jesuit general, roughly one month before his death — appointed him as provincial superior of Germany. That included the Catholic parts of Germany (Swabia, Bavaria, Bohemia) and Austria as well as Hungary. For the next fourteen years, he served as German provincial, representing Catholics in dialogues with the Protestants at

Regensburg (1556–1557) and Worms (1557) and even living for seven years (1559-1566) in Augsburg, where he served as cathedral preacher. He briefly returned to the Council of Trent as a theological expert in May 1562, but came back to Augsburg early when the Protestants took advantage of his absence to torment local Catholics.

Canisius remained humble despite his fame. Recalling the opinion of St. Ignatius that ingratitude is the worst of all sins, and reflecting on the gratitude he owed God for his vocation, St. Peter Canisius's prayer Wash Me with Your Precious Blood communicates his desire to give everything back to the Lord out of love:

> See, O merciful God, what return
> I, your thankless servant, have made
> for the innumerable favors
> and the wonderful love you have shown me!
> What wrongs I have done, what good left undone!
> Wash away, I beg you, these faults and stains
> with your precious blood, most kind Redeemer,
> and make up for my poverty by applying your merits.
> Give me the protection I need to amend my life.
> I give and surrender myself wholly to you,
> and offer you all I possess,
> with the prayer that you bestow your grace on me,
> so that I may be able to devote and employ
> all the thinking power of my mind
> and the strength of my body in your holy service,
> who are God blessed for ever and ever. Amen.

Practically alone among the first generation of Jesuits, Fr. Canisius's ministry continued for decades, and he outlived most of his peers to become a wisdom figure in the Society of Jesus. From 1580 to 1589, he founded St. Michael College at Fribourg, Switzerland, where he continued to preach weekly at St. Nicholas parish. But in spring 1589, health issues finally slowed him down, and he suffered a stroke in 1591 at the age of seventy that forced him to use a cane. Undaunted, he continued to prepare Catholic manuscripts for the printing press that he had learned to use with an effectiveness equal to that of Martin Luther's disciples.

In September 1597, Canisius suddenly contracted a perfect storm of illnesses — dropsy, lung congestion, and ulcers in his throat — that left him unable to say Mass. In this state, on December 21 of that year, he died peacefully in his sleep at seventy-six. And while St. Ignatius of Loyola did not found the Society of Jesus with the express purpose of advancing the Counter-Reformation, Canisius reminds us that he committed Jesuits to this mission very early. St. Peter Canisius, priest and Doctor of the Church, pray for us.

St. Robert Bellarmine

Before Cardinal Jorge Mario Bergoglio, S.J., was elected as Pope Francis in March 2013, only one Jesuit cardinal had ever been in danger of becoming pope — and he came very close indeed.

St. Robert Bellarmine (1542–1621), cardinal and Doctor of the Church, entered the Society at eighteen and overlapped with St. Peter Canisius in the order for the last thirty-seven years of the latter's life. But unlike Fr. Canisius, who dealt primarily with poorly catechized Catholics on the German front of the Reformation, Cardinal Bellarmine lived and taught for most of his life in his native Italy — a land where educated people continued to practice Catholicism even as the rest of Europe wavered in it. Widely considered the most learned theologian of the Roman Church in his lifetime, Cardinal Bellarmine spent much of his career resisting the honors that others tried to heap on him, including ultimately the papacy itself.

Born in the Tuscan village of Montepulciano, young Robert had the misfortune of being the nephew of Pope Marcellus II, raising expectations for his future. In 1557, the year after St. Ignatius's death, he transferred as a teenager from the local grammar school to a new Jesuit school in his town. Admiring the humility and zeal of his Jesuit teachers there, and expressing a desire to join their company, he overcame his father's resistance after his family made a unique arrangement with Fr. General James Lainez: To test the sincerity of his vocation, young Robert would live at home for one year, counting it as his novitiate if he endured. Of course, the year passed without a problem, and Robert duly presented himself before Fr. General Lainez in Rome to pronounce his first vows in the fall of 1560.

After two weeks at the Jesuit generalate, Robert studied philosophy at the Roman College (now the Pontifical Gregorian University) from 1560 to 1563. He then spent the next two years teaching in Florence and Mondovi, where he preached in the city's cathedral despite not yet being ordained. A gifted speaker and writer, Robert continued to preach during his theology studies at the University of Padua from 1567 to 1569, and at the University of Louvain in Belgium, where he transferred for his final year of theology.

After his priestly ordination in May 1570, at the age of twenty-seven, Fr. Bellarmine became the first theology professor at the newly opened Jesuit theologate in Louvain. Over the next several years in this job, he familiarized himself with the writings of leading Protestant reformers and answered their objections to Roman Catholicism in his classes. His success with this method led his Jesuit superiors to summon him back to Rome in 1576, where he became the first chairman of controversial theology at the Roman

College, summarizing theological disputes with Protestants and giving extended explanations of the Roman Catholic perspective in his classes. For eleven years, Fr. Bellarmine's lectures were wildly popular with students, and the Holy Father appointed him to papal commissions to revise the Vulgate Latin Bible and produce a new edition of the Septuagint Greek Bible.

During his time at the Roman College, Fr. Bellarmine also published several major treatises on controversial theology, defending papal authority with a forcefulness that attracted both Catholic and Protestant readers. In 1588, he stopped teaching to finish this writing, but continued to serve as spiritual director for the Jesuit seminarians, including St. Aloysius Gonzaga. It was with a heavy heart that he watched Aloysius die while helping plague victims.

In 1592, Fr. Bellarmine became rector for all 220 Jesuits at the Roman College. Continuing his meteoric rise, the Jesuit general then appointed him provincial superior of the Jesuits in Naples from 1594 to 1596, a role he fulfilled to the letter until Pope Clement VIII appointed him to replace a deceased Jesuit cardinal as the papal theological adviser. As rector and provincial, he had made special efforts to visit everyone in his care as often as possible, but the pope pulled him back into writing and speaking.

After publishing a popular catechism in 1598, Fr. Bellarmine found himself rumored for a cardinal's red hat, leading him and Fr. General Claudio Aquaviva to do everything they could to prevent him from getting it. As Pope Francis knows, St. Ignatius of Loyola requires fully professed Jesuits to renounce ecclesiastical honors, refusing to become bishops or cardinals — or pope — unless the Church insists on it. In this case, Bellarmine and Aquaviva were unable to talk the pope out of honoring the great theologian. Yet despite being named a cardinal in March 1599, Bellarmine led a disinterested and ascetic life of research among the servants and carriages of his new office, rejecting gifts and distributing his monthly surplus to Rome's poor.

The pope surprised Cardinal Bellarmine again by appointing him archbishop of Capua from 1602 to 1605, a job he fulfilled with the same pastoral zeal he had displayed as provincial of Naples, spending time with his people and visiting each ministry personally. In the spring of 1605, he voted in the papal conclave that elected Leo XI. When this pope died one month later and Bellarmine attended his second conclave in the span of a year, he was horrified to find himself a leading candidate to be the next pope.

Echoing a sentiment that Cardinal Bergoglio undoubtedly felt in the conclave of 2013, Cardinal Bellarmine reportedly prayed: "From the papacy, deliver me, O Lord!" While Bergoglio was not quite so lucky, Cardinal Bellarmine breathed a sigh of relief when the cardinals eventually passed him over as too impractical and bookish to be pope, and he happily accepted compromise appointments to several Vatican congregations.

The Grateful Cardinal

Much as Pope Francis did by visiting Jesuit headquarters after his election, and by visiting the homeless in Buenos Aires when he was a cardinal, St. Robert Bellarmine worked hard to remain a faithful Jesuit amidst all of these honors. Even as a cardinal, he lived his vows with humility and continued to make an annual eight-day Ignatian retreat that he soon expanded into an annual thirty-day retreat. Scholarly even at prayer, he wrote three works of spiritual theology during these retreats, including *On the Ascent of the Mind to God* (1614). In the second reading for Matins in the Divine Office on his feast day, we find this excerpt from that book:

Incline my heart to your decrees.

Sweet Lord, you are meek and merciful. Who would not give himself wholeheartedly to your service, if he began to taste even a little of your fatherly rule? What command, Lord, do you give your servants? *Take my yoke upon you,* you say. And what is this yoke of yours like? *My yoke,* you say, *is easy and my burden light.* Who would not be glad to bear a yoke that does not press hard but caresses? Who would not be glad for a burden that does not weigh heavy but refreshes? And so you were right to add: *And you will find rest for your souls.* And what is this yoke of yours that does not weary, but gives rest? It is, of course, that first and greatest commandment: *You shall love the Lord your God with all your heart.* What is easier, sweeter, more pleasant, than to love goodness, beauty and love, the fullness of which you are, O Lord, my God?

Is it not true that you promise those who keep your commandments a reward more desirable than great wealth and sweeter than honey? You promise a most abundant reward, for as your apostle James says: *The Lord has prepared a crown of life for those who love him.* What is this crown of life? It is surely a greater good than we can conceive of or desire, as Saint Paul says, quoting Isaiah: *Eye has not seen, ear has not heard, nor has it so much as dawned on man what God has prepared for those who love him.*

Truly then the recompense is great for those who keep your commandments. That first and greatest commandment helps the man who obeys, not the God who commands. In addition, the other commandments of God perfect the man who obeys them. They provide him with what he needs. They instruct and enlighten him and make him good and blessed. If you are wise, then, know that you have been created for the glory of God and your own eternal salvation. This is your goal; this is the center of your life; this is the treasure of your heart. If you reach this goal, you will find happiness. If you fail to reach it, you will find misery.

May you consider truly good whatever leads to your goal and truly evil whatever makes you fall away from it. Prosperity and adversity, wealth and poverty, health and sickness, honors and humiliations, life and death, in the mind of the wise man, are not to be sought for their own sake, nor avoided for their own sake. But if they contribute to the glory of God and your eternal happiness, then they are good and should be sought. If they detract from this, they are evil and must be avoided.

These uplifting words, taken from the cardinal's writings during his annual retreat experience of the Spiritual Exercises, reflect a deeply Ignatian gratitude for all that "God has prepared for those who love him." Yet because he was so skillful at handling theological controversies for the Vatican, including debates with King James I over the indirect spiritual authority of the papacy versus the Anglican-coined "divine right of kings," Cardinal Bellarmine found himself repeatedly drawn into hot-button conflicts. In 1616, he got involved in the Copernican controversy, admonishing Galileo Galilei (1564–1642) in a letter not to publicly defend or hold the theory that the earth revolves around the sun until Rome could be sure Catholics would not lose their faith over it.

Because most seventeenth-century Europeans believed in the pagan Ptolemaic cosmology that saw the sun revolving around the earth at the universe's center, and had come to appropriate this fact as a proof text for the Bible's worldview, Cardinal Bellarmine thought he was defending the harmony of faith and science by asking Galileo not to teach his findings until theology caught up with them. Galileo obeyed and died as a good Catholic, with his daughter becoming a nun, but he suffered greatly from the agreement to censor his work. In 1992, Pope St. John Paul II officially exonerated and apologized to Galileo on behalf of the Roman Catholic Church, recognizing that the Vatican had mistreated the great astronomer in a way that inadvertently chilled scientific inquiry in Catholic circles.

In the last years of his life, the great Cardinal Bellarmine grew tired of controversy and asked several times to retire to the Jesuit novitiate in Rome, where he might return to the simplicity of community life that he had missed so deeply since becoming cardinal. Multiple popes, seeing his presence at the Vatican as essential, refused this request. But Gregory XV finally allowed it when the cardinal's hearing loss and frailty became so obvious that even casual observers could see Bellarmine was running on fumes.

As with many elderly people today, to whom any change in routine can be fatal after a certain age, Cardinal Bellarmine declined rapidly in this final transition. Arriving at the novitiate of Sant'Andrea on August 21, 1621, he was struck down by a lethal fever three days later. As he clung to life for two weeks, the pope and cardinals came to ask for his prayers, touching their skullcaps and pectoral crosses to his head and chest to keep as relics. On the morning of September 17, now his feast day, St. Robert Bellarmine died peacefully as he softly repeated: "Jesus, Jesus, Jesus!"

Although the great cardinal had asked to have a simple funeral and be buried at the feet of St. Aloysius Gonzaga, the holy Jesuit scholastic who died under his spiritual care while ministering to plague victims thirty years earlier, the pope refused to allow it. Instead, he ordered a grand public funeral for the famed Jesuit scholar. The body of St. Robert Bellarmine, patron saint of catechists, now lies in repose at the Church of St. Ignatius in Rome.

In 1 Corinthians 12, St. Paul says there is one Holy Spirit who bestows many gifts upon us. Saints Margaret Mary Alacoque, Claude La Colombière, Peter Canisius, and Robert Bellarmine come down to us as very different people. They had distinct personalities, gifts, and experiences. But in their own way, each practiced a key Ignatian spiritual virtue that Pope Francis himself maintains: In the midst of life's daily challenges, they gazed in gratitude at Jesus Christ.

TRANSFORMATION

Our hope is Jesus; it is only Jesus.
— Pope Francis, homily to Jesuits, September 27, 2014

When Jesus Christ walked on earth, some people paid attention to him, but most did not. It remains the same today. Many good and holy Christians, including even members of the clergy, spend our days contemplating everything from politics to water bills. The one thing we rarely contemplate is God or the saints who lead us to him.

Some of us take God for granted. If we pay, pray, and obey, we assume we will never suffer or struggle with anything in life. When something bad happens, we tell others we have become atheists or agnostics, but the truth is we were already those things for a long time, even at Sunday Mass. We may not have noticed it, but our relationship with God depended on the unspoken agreement that Jesus would stay at arm's length if we performed our external obligations.

Rather than let Jesus draw close to us in all the joy and pain of a real relationship, we learn to talk about this relationship impersonally, paying lip service to our savior in the same way we might wave at a homeless man without actually stopping to converse.

Even Christians who claim to have a "personal relationship with Jesus" often seem better at talking *about* it than at speaking *with* and listening *to* Jesus. When we try to pray with Scriptures or pay attention to the presence of Jesus in the people and events of our daily lives, we frequently end up *analyzing* the Lord more than *experiencing* him. We sit with our Bibles and think *about* him, but we do not actually talk *to* him or simply *be with* him as with a friend, so we end up trying to control or tell him what to do instead of contemplating his face or listening for his voice.

Ignatian spirituality, too, can get in our way when it immerses us in jargon. Technical terms like "first week," "annotation," and "colloquy" may serve as uncomfortable reminders that St. Ignatius wrote the Spiritual Exercises as a handbook for *directors* rather than as a do-it-yourself guide to prayer for individuals. Newcomers to Ignatian spirituality often find themselves frustrated with the number of books and guides on this topic that make them feel like they need a class on "Jesuit speak" just to pray.

St. Ignatius of Loyola, though he intended the Exercises as a spirituality to be *experienced* on retreat or in spiritual direction more than *taught* academically, can also get in our way when he speaks in sixteenth-century terms that don't feel helpful. That's why he encouraged retreat directors to adapt the Exercises to different persons and contexts, taking what is helping and leaving the rest. Today, as we look at the example of Pope Francis, we can see this principle of adaptation in action. Reflecting on the Jesuit saints and on other saints, as we have done in this book, we can get a sense of the deeper movements of the Spirit that drive the heart of a man like Francis.

We Jesuits, coming from a religious order named "The Society of Jesus," devote our prayer to immitating Jesus first and foremost. We seek to find God in all things, by which we mean the specific circumstances and events of our daily lives rather than a generic "God is everywhere" slogan devoid of meaningful content. By God, we typically mean Jesus, the one and only savior who manifests the Holy Trinity, and we can only encounter him in prayer through our thoughts and feelings in the present moment.

Many Jesuit saints exemplify the Christ-like virtues of trust, openness, generosity, simplicity, dedication, and gratitude. While these qualities are not mutually exclusive, I have tried to highlight particular saints for each of these virtues in the chapters of this book. I have looked at the deep trust of saints such as Francis Xavier in traveling to an unknown culture alone, the openness of saints such as John Berchmans in following God's will even when it clashed with family expectations, and the generosity of saints such as the Japanese martyrs who gave their very lives for Christ.

I have looked at the simplicity of saints like Alphonsus Rodriguez who found Jesus in their routine, at the dedication of the North American martyrs, who refused to give up on their people, and at the gratitude of saints such as Claude La Colombière who gave thanks to God even in the midst of great internal and external suffering. I have looked at non-Jesuit saints, such as Kateri Tekakwitha and Margaret Mary Alacoque, who found God alongside these saintly Jesuits.

All of these Jesuit saints, like Pope Francis, share the fundamental virtue of humility that allowed them to place the entire hope of their lives into the hands of Jesus Christ. Praying over the images of these saints' lives in our imaginations, we might wish to contemplate the One who inspired their lives and who now invites us to live in the hope of a better world where we will meet all of them united before God's throne. At Mass on the Solemnity of All Saints each year, the Roman Catholic Church listens to these words of St. John from his vision of the saints in heaven:

> Then I saw another angel come up from the East, holding the seal of the living God. He cried out in a loud voice to the four angels who were given power to damage the land and the sea, "Do not damage the land or the sea or the trees until we put the

seal on the foreheads of the servants of our God." I heard the number of those who had been marked with the seal, one hundred and forty-four thousand marked from every tribe of the Israelites....

After this I had a vision of a great multitude, which no one could count, from every nation, race, people, and tongue. They stood before the throne and before the Lamb, wearing white robes and holding palm branches in their hands. They cried out in a loud voice:

> "Salvation comes from our God,
>   who is seated on the throne,
> and from the Lamb."

All the angels stood around the throne and around the elders and the four living creatures. They prostrated themselves before the throne, worshiped God, and exclaimed:

> "Amen. Blessing and glory, wisdom
>   and thanksgiving,
> honor, power, and might
> be to our God forever and ever.
> Amen."

Then one of the elders spoke up and said to me, "Who are these wearing white robes, and where did they come from?" I said to him, "My lord, you are the one who knows." He said to me, "These are the ones who have survived the time of great distress; they have washed their robes and made them white in the Blood of the Lamb."

(Revelation 7:2–4, 9–14)

According to St. John's vision, all Christians who suffer for our faith — enduring ridicule, doubt, fear, imprisonment, torture, and even death for love of Jesus — will be washed in the Lord's blood and made white as snow before the Lamb in heaven. In St. John's time, the "great distress" that claimed the lives of so many saints was the persecution of Domitian and other Roman emperors, but today Christians can fill in this meaning with our own sufferings. All of us make great sacrifices to remain faithful in our broken twenty-first century, where extreme poverty coexists with extreme luxury. Yet Jesus Christ remains among us, waiting for us to place him at the center of our hearts.

In this context, the Book of Revelation remains a message for Christians of all times, promising that God will reward us if we hold fast to our faith even in times of difficulty, just as the saints before us did. In his homily on the above reading at the Cemetery of Verano for All Saints' Day on November 1, 2013, Pope Francis said the saints who have already been washed in the blood of Christ give us hope of heaven:

> We can enter heaven only thanks to the blood of the Lamb, thanks to the blood of Christ. Christ's own blood has justified us, which has opened for us the gates of heaven. And if today we remember our brothers and sisters who have gone before us in life and are in Heaven, it is because they have been washed in the blood of Christ. This is our hope: the hope of Christ's blood! It is a hope that does not disappoint. If we walk with the Lord in life, he will never disappoint us!

As Catholics, we turn to the saints not merely as good examples but as intercessors who pray for us constantly from heaven. When our loved ones die, and we continue to talk with them as we fall asleep each night, we pray *for* them to get to heaven, but we also pray *to* them for their help and protection in case they are already there. If they suffered for their faith, and if we continue to suffer today, we must remember that "the souls of the righteous are in the hand of God" (Wisdom 3:1) — with Jesus Christ — who suffered and died as one of us.

Four days after the entire Roman Catholic Church celebrates the saints on All Saints' Day, including both those saints who are canonized and those who are not, the Society of Jesus commemorates our own beatified and canonized members. The collect for the Feast of All Saints and Blessed of the Society of Jesus, November 5, asks our Heavenly Father for the grace to follow his Son as "good soldiers" in the work of salvation:

> Lord God, Father of our Lord Jesus Christ,
> you call us to your service though you know how weak
> we are.
> Help us to be good soldiers of Christ under the banner of
> his cross.
> Bring to perfection the work you have begun in St. Ignatius
> and so many of his followers,
> now acclaimed as saints and blessed.
> We ask this through our Lord Jesus Christ, your Son,
> who lives and reigns with you and the Holy Spirit, one God,
> for ever and ever. Amen.

Of course, we are not saints yet, and the Lord invites all of us to grow in holiness through prayer, which remains the primary way we communicate with him and have a relationship. To be in relationship with someone requires listening as well as speaking. So for readers who have read this far, and who feel like trying out a little Ignatian prayer, I want to leave you with a contemplation exercise to try on your own. In this next section, I have provided a Scripture passage, but you are welcome to use this template with any Gospel passage you wish to pray over. If you do not find yourself drawn to Jesus in this passage, you might also draw close to one of his disciples, the saints.

Ignatian Contemplation Exercise

Find a quiet, comfortable place to spend one hour in silent prayer. Spread out and stay away from others as much as possible, choosing a spot free of distractions. Then follow the instructions below, going from step to step as the Holy Spirit moves you.

Opening: Make the Sign of the Cross. Sit comfortably, neither slouching nor rigid, and recall that you are in God's loving presence.

- Relax your body, focusing on God's presence within, around, and beyond you. You may find it helpful to breathe deeply for a few moments (St. Robert Bellarmine suggests that you inhale the Holy Spirit, hold your breath briefly, and exhale worries and distractions as you tune in to God), repeat a prayerful phrase in your head, sing a favorite hymn·verse to yourself, or pray a decade of the Rosary. Be patient with yourself until you feel relaxed, centered, and focused on the Lord.

Preparatory prayer: Spiritual Exercises [46] — "to ask God our Lord that all my intentions, actions, and operations may be directed purely to the service and praise of His Divine Majesty."

- Greet the Lord and tell him this prayer period is totally dedicated to him and to his desires for you.

Now read this passage once to get a feel for it:

The Calming of the Storm at Sea — Matthew 8:23–27: He got into a boat and his disciples followed him. Suddenly a violent storm came up on the sea, so that the boat was being swamped by waves; but he was asleep. They came and woke him, saying, "Lord, save us! We are perishing!" He said to them, "Why are you terrified, O you of little faith?" Then he got up, rebuked the winds and the sea, and there was great calm. The men were amazed and said, "What sort of man is this, whom even the winds and the sea obey?"

- What strikes you about this passage? What line or image jumps out at you when you read it? Focus on that part of the text.

First prelude: [47] — "a composition, seeing the place."

- Imagine yourself in this Gospel story: Place yourself among the disciples as one of them or as yourself. Where do you see yourself? Are you close to Jesus or far away?

- Who is with you? What do their faces look like? What do their voices sound like?

- What else do you see, hear, taste, smell, and touch? What do you notice about Jesus and the disciples who are with you? Etc.

Second prelude: [48] — "to ask God our Lord for what I want and desire."

- Example from the Spiritual Exercises: Ask God for the grace [104] to know Jesus more clearly, to love him more dearly, and to follow him more nearly.

- Or you may ask for another grace if there is something else you desire from God.

- What matters is that you ask the Lord *from your heart* for what you desire right now.

Contemplation: Read the passage again slowly, imagining you are part of it and that every word is directed to you. What are the people in the story feeling and thinking as it unfolds? What is Jesus feeling? What feelings and thoughts arise in you?

Let the Holy Spirit guide your prayer as you allow your attention to settle on one particular image in the scene.

Colloquy: [54] "The Colloquy is made, properly speaking, as one friend speaks to another."

- Near the hour's end, picture yourself alone with Jesus, looking at him as he looks at you.

- Tell Jesus what happened in the hour: Say where you felt peaceful, scared, frustrated, happy, alive, lonely, etc. Share any memories, desires, thoughts, or questions that came up for you. Tell him everything that stirred inside you, even if it felt like a distraction.

- Listen and watch for the Lord's response. Does Jesus answer you through a word or phrase from the passage? What is he like with you? How does he feel about you?

Formally end the prayer hour by saying the Our Father (or another favorite written prayer) with feeling and making the Sign of the Cross. Then write down what happened.

Go in Peace

There are many saints in our lives, living and dead, who have befriended the Lord through this kind of prayer. They are our friends, too. We talk to them when we need support or when we struggle with our faith. We look to them as models for drawing close to Jesus in our own prayer.

To pray in this way is fundamentally "de-centering," as it requires us to step aside and let Jesus Christ take front stage, inviting him to steer the boat of our lives. Pope Francis remains free to be himself, loving God and others as himself, precisely because Jesus (and no one else) occupies the center of his attention. Jesus is Lord, not us, but he is also our friend and companion on the journey.

All of the Jesuit saints lead us to Jesus, the constant companion of their lives, when we reflect on their stories. Contemplating the Jesuit saints in prayer, we feel drawn to contemplate the loving presence beyond them, the Love that sustained them and helped them endure unspeakable sufferings in their lifetimes. Only this Presence can transform us into the grateful persons, and the people, we find ourselves called to be.

We have been created for a purpose greater than anything we see with the naked eye. We have been created to love, reverence, and serve God our Lord, and by this means to save our souls. All other things lead to this one goal.

In the end there remains only one image we need to ponder deep in our hearts when we wake up in the morning, when we go to work, and when the lights go out at night. All the pope's saints gaze upon it with us. Jesus, Jesus, Jesus.

ALSO BY SEAN SALAI, S.J.

What Would Pope Francis Do?
Bringing the Good News to People in Need
(ID# T1727)

Pope Francis has insistently invited all of us to live passionate lives of faith and encounter, in particular reaching out to the poor, the lost, the lonely, and anyone who, for whatever reason, is on the margins of society. Taking six themes from Pope Francis's apostolic exhortation *Evangelii Gaudium*, **What Would Pope Francis Do?** examines the essence of our mission and the movements of the heart that allow us to go boldly toward those on the peripheries to build a better world.

Available from Our Sunday Visitor.
Visit osv.com or call 800-348-2440.